9789876543213165498765544322132246509870987341240923874091387401298374012392874 0123928740
19238754093825672945857210293830498712304872308472023985750987609831723098472103
98747209387474710923470198374508349659543561435600189437502913847409856734891675
49087340293470892570459874045873140958743058971048574988765431324679876546554313
21313467897324321301983740291837427386481274208474309387402193865724365287978987
65432131654987655443221322465098709873412409238740913874012983740123928740192387
5409382567293049871230487230847202398575098760983172309847210398747209387474585 7
21029384710923470198374508349659543561435600189437502913847409856734891675490873
40293470892570459304987123048723084720239857509876609831723098472103987472093874 8
74045873140958743058971048574988765431324679876546554313213134678973243213019837
4029183742738648127420847433049871230487230847202398575098760983172309847210398 7
47209387470938740219386572436528797898765432131654987655443221322465098709873412
40923874091387401298374012392874019238754093825672945857210293847109234701983745
08349659543561435600189437502913847409856734891675490873402934708925704598740458
73140958743058971048574988765431324679876546554313213134678973243213019837402918
37427386481274208474309387402193865724365287978987654321316549876554432213224650
98709873412409238740913874012983740123928740192387540938256729458572102938471092
34701983745083496595435614356001894375029138474098567348916754908734029347089257
04598740458731409587430589710485749887654313246798765465543132131346789732432130
19837402918374273864812742084743093874021938657243652879789876543213165498765544
32213224650987098734124092387409138740129837401239287401923875409382567294585721
02938471092347019837450834965954356143560018943750291384740985673489167549087340
29347089257045987404587314095874305897104857498876543132467987654655431321313467
89732432130198374029183742738648127420847430938740219386572436528797898765432131
65498765544322132246509870987341240923874091387401298374012392874019238754093825
67294585721029384710923470198374508349659543561435600189437502913847409856734891
67549087340293470892570459874045873140958743058971048574988765431324679876546554
31321313467897324321301983740291837427386481274208474309387402193865724365287304
98712304872308472023985750987612742084743093874021938657243652879789876543213165
49876554432213224650987098734124092387409138740129837401239287401923875409382567
29458572102938471092347019837450812742084743093874021938657243652879789876543213
16549876554432213224650987098734124092387409138740129837401239287401923875409382
56729458572102938471092347019837450834965954356143560018943409238740913874012983
74012392874019238754093825672945857210293847109234701983745083496595752913847409
85673489167549087340293470892570459874045873496595435614356001894375013847409856
43213019837402918374273864812742084743093874021938657243652873049871230487230847

9789876543213165498765544322132246509870987341240923874091387401298374012392874 0
192387540938256729458572102938304987123048723084720239857509876098317230984721 03
987472093874747109234701983745083496595435614356001894375029138474098567348916 75
490873402934708925704598740458731409587430589710485749887654313246798765465543 13
213134678973243213019837402918374273864812742084743093874021938657243652879789 87
654321316549876554432213224650987098734124092387409138740129837401239287401923 87
540938256729304987123048723084720239857509876098317230984721039874720938747458 57
210293847109234701983745083496595435614356001894375029138474098567348916754908 73
402934708925704593049871230487230847202398575098760983172309847210398747209387 48
740458731409587430589710485749887654313246798765465543132131346789732432130198 37
402918374273864812742084743304987123048723084720239857509876098317230984721039 87
472093874709387402193865724365287978987654321316549876554432213224650987098734 12
409238740913874012983740123928740192387540938256729458572102938471092347019837 45
083496595435614356001894375029138474098567348916754908734029347089257045987404 58
731409587430589710485749887654313246798765465543132131346789732432130198374029 18
374273864812742084743093874021938657243652879789876543213165498765544322132246 50
987098734124092387409138740129837401239287401923875409382567294585721029384710 92
347019837450834965954356143560018943750291384740985673489167549087340293470892 57
045987404587314095874305897104857498876543132467987654655431321313467897324321 30
198374029183742738648127420847430938740219386572436528797898765432131654987655 44
322132246509870987341240923874091387401298374012392874019238754093825672945857 21
029384710923470198374508349659543561435600189437502913847409856734891675490873 40
293470892570459874045873140958743058971048574988765431324679876546554313213134 67
897324321301983740291837427386481274208474309387402193865724365287978987654321 31
654987655443221322465098709873412409238740913874012983740123928740192387540938 25
672945857210293847109234701983745083496595435614356001894375029138474098567348 91
675490873402934708925704598740458731409587430589710485749887654313246798765465 54
313213134678973243213019837402918374273864812742084743093874021938657243652873 04
987123048723084720239857509876127420847430938740219386572436528797898765432131 65
498765544322132246509870987341240923874091387401298374012392874019238754093825 67
294585721029384710923470198374508127420847430938740219386572436528797898765432 13
165498765544322132246509870987341240923874091387401298374012392874019238754093 82
567294585721029384710923470198374508349659543561435600189434092387409138740129 83
740123928740192387540938256729458572102938471092347019837450834965975291384740 9
856734891675490873402934708925704598740458734965954356143560018943750138474098 56
432130198374029183742738648127420847430938740219386572436528730498712304872308 47

978987654321316549876554432213224650987098734124092387409138740129837401239 28740
192387540938256729458572102938304987123048723084720239857509876098317230984 72103
987472093874747109234701983745083496595435614356001894375029138474098567348 91675
490873402934708925704598740458731409587430589710485749887654313246798765465 54313
213134678973243213019837402918374273864812742084743093874021938657243652879 78987
654321316549876554432213224650987098734124092387409138740129837401239287401 92387
540938256729304987123048723084720239857509876098317230984721039874720938747 45857
210293847109234701983745083496595435614356001894375029138474098567348916754 90873
402934708925704593049871230487230847202398575098760983172309847210398747209 38748
740458731409587430589710485749887654313246798765465554313213134678973243213 019837
402918374273864812742084743304987123048723084720239857509876098317230984721 03987
472093874709387402193865724365287978987654321316549876554432213224650987098 73412
409238740913874012983740123928740192387540938256729458572102938471092347019 83745
083496595435614356001894375029138474098567348916754908734029347089257045987 40458
731409587430589710485749887654313246798765465554313213134678973243213019837 402918
374273864812742084743093874021938657243652879789876543213165498765544322132 24650
987098734124092387409138740129837401239287401923875409382567294585721029384 71092
347019837450834965954356143560018943750291384740985673489167549087340293470 89257
045987404587314095874305897104857498876543132467987654655431321313467897324 32130
198374029183742738648127420847430938740219386572436528797898765432131654987 65544
322132246509870987341240923874091387401298374012392874019238754093825672945 85721
029384710923470198374508349659543561435600189437502913847409856734891675490 87340
293470892570459874045873140958743058971048574988765431324679876546554313213 13467
897324321301983740291837427386481274208474309387402193865724365287978987654 32131
654987655443221322465098709873412409238740913874012983740123928740192387540 93825
672945857210293847109234701983745083496595435614356001894375029138474098567 34891
675490873402934708925704598740458731409587430589710485749887654313246798765 46554
313213134678973243213019837402918374273864812742084743093874021938657243652 87304
987123048723084720239857509876127420847430938740219386572436528797898765432 13165
498765544322132246509870987341240923874091387401298374012392874019238754093 82567
294585721029384710923470198374508127420847430938740219386572436528797898765 43213
165498765544322132246509870987341240923874091387401298374012392874019238754 09382
567294585721029384710923470198374508349659543561435600189434092387409138740 12983
740123928740192387540938256729458572102938471092347019837450834965957529138 47409
856734891675490873402934708925704598740458734965954356143560018943750138474 09856
432130198374029183742738648127420847430938740219386572436528730498712304872 30847

9789876543213165498765544322132246509870987341240923874091387401298374012392 8740
192387540938256729458572102938304987123048723084720239857509876098317230984 72103
987472093874747109234701983745083496595435614356001894375029138474098567348 91675
490873402934708925704598740458731409587430589710485749887654313246798765465 54313
213134678973243213019837402918374273864812742084743093874021938657243652879 78987
654321316549876554432213224650987098734124092387409138740129837401239287401 92387
540938256729304987123048723084720239857509876098317230984721039874720938747 45857
210293847109234701983745083496595435614356001894375029138474098567348916754 90873
402934708925704593049871230487230847202398575098760983172309847210398747209 38748
740458731409587430589710485749887654313246798765465543132131346789732432130 19837
402918374273864812742084743304987123048723084720239857509876098317230984721 03987
472093874709387402193865724365287978987654321316549876554432213224650987098 73412
409238740913874012983740123928740192387540938256729458572102938471092347019 83745
083496595435614356001894375029138474098567348916754908734029347089257045987 40458
731409587430589710485749887654313246798765465543132131346789732432130198374 02918
374273864812742084743093874021938657243652879789876543213165498765544322132 24650
987098734124092387409138740129837401239287401923875409382567294585721029384 71092
347019837450834965954356143560018943750291384740985673489167549087340293470 89257
045987404587314095874305897104857498876543132467987654655431321313467897324 32130
198374029183742738648127420847430938740219386572436528797898765432131654987 65544
322132246509870987341240923874091387401298374012392874019238754093825672945 85721
029384710923470198374508349659543561435600189437502913847409856734891675490 87340
293470892570459874045873140958743058971048574988765431324679876546554313213 13467
897324321301983740291837427386481274208474309387402193865724365287978987654 32131
654987655443221322465098709873412409238740913874012983740123928740192387540 93825
672945857210293847109234701983745083496595435614356001894375029138474098567 34891
675490873402934708925704598740458731409587430589710485749887654313246798765 46554
313213134678973243213019837402918374273864812742084743093874021938657243652 87304
987123048723084720239857509876127420847430938740219386572436528797898765432 13165
498765544322132246509870987341240923874091387401298374012392874019238754093 82567
294585721029384710923470198374508127420847430938740219386572436528797898765 43213
165498765544322132246509870987341240923874091387401298374012392874019238754 09382
567294585721029384710923470198374508349659543561435600189434092387409138740 12983
740123928740192387540938256729458572102938471092347019837450834965957529138 47409
856734891675490873402934708925704598740458734965954356143560018943750138474 09856
432130198374029183742738648127420847430938740219386572436528730498712304872 30847

THE NUMBERS

GORDON MASSMAN

PAVEMENT SAW PRESS

OHIO   2000

The following poems first appeared, or are forthcoming in the following periodicals:

Another Chicago Magazine, Antioch Review, Artful Dodge, Atom Mind, Black Dirt, Confrontation, Connecticut Poetry Review, Contemporary Voice 2 (Canada), Cortland Review, The Fiddlehead (Canada), 5 AM, Flyway, The Georgia Review, Green Mountains Review, Greensboro Review, The Harvard Review, Hiram Poetry Review, Iron (UK), Karamu, Many Mountains Moving, Membrane, Men's Council Journal, The New York Quarterly, Left Curve, Libido, Lingo, The Literary Review, Old Crow Review, Paperplates (Canada), Pavement Saw, Penny Dreadful, Pleiades, Prairie Journal (Canada), Prism International (Canada), Quarter After Eight, Rattle, Response, Third Coast, Willow Springs, The Windless Orchard, Windsor Review (Canada), and Yellow Silk.
Cover Design: Polly Christensen

The editor, David Baratier, gives accolades to Gordon Massman for his twenty years spent producing this work; as well as Polly Christensen, Jane Schill and Steve Mainard who have donated time to this endeavor. Gordon Massman thanks David Joel for his friendship and perseverance. The author would also like to thank the editors of the publications these poems first appeared in.

Pavement Saw Press
PO Box 6291
Columbus, OH 43206

Ohio Arts Council
A STATE AGENCY
THAT SUPPORTS PUBLIC
PROGRAMS IN THE ARTS

Products are available through the publisher or through:
Small Press Distribution / 1341 Seventh St. / Berkeley, CA 94710 / 510.524.1668

For Sue Ellen

A splinter in the eye is the best magnifying glass.

--Theodore Adorno

Then you have become a language on my tongue--
silver and blue and ruby and almond syllabics,
like liquid, slipping from that secret place--
jungle crease or lubricated jewel--where words are born
onto the rushing river of my life, and
though love is the razor that slits the throat
I continue to grip it in my hand.
I speak the rune of foreignness, letters stripped off
ancient scripts and stung into my head--
"gratification," "giving," "sacrifice,"
"gentleness," "patience," "desire"--
words I used not in their manifest meaning
before touching you now flow through me like oil from a tun.
What did I speak for truth before fulfillment?
What tools did I implement?
Loneliness perverts the word, twists it
into a spike of rage or guilt or hopelessness
and how we raise it in our halls into a God.
Dipped in you, you drip off me in a clarity of vision,
shifting the kaleidoscope not into another
configuration of need, but dismantling the toy--
eyehole, tube, and all--opening a window
and scattering the stones like a handful of bird seed.
I feel clean. Love is more than dominance
in bed. To see through its crystal sea for
more than an instant is to be blessed past
the blindness which grips us all. To see
the burst and flash of truth through hazy eyes....
You come to me more than in the limits
of your skin--seam of thumb (often winter-split),
stitch of eye, or fist of knee--but in immensity
peeled open, broken, spattered--like light itself
pouring through a universe. Love is the razor
that slits the throat and in my hand
I squeeze its edge in the moment of unbefuddlement.
And words pour forth: "hammer," and "tooth,"
and "indiscriminate;" "street," and "structure,"
and "bewilderment;" "horse," and "bird,"
and "disfigurement;" and, in the plexus of human love,
the word "civilization," the power of whose meaning
I could not have known until now.

To lay a sheet of light over a sheet of dark
over a sheet of light over a sheet of dark
like a pastry formed of filo dough, light,dark,
light,dark,light,dark until the whole personality
is included, sadness over joy over love over shame,
to lay sheet over sheet of flaky delicacy
so easily hurt and devoured, yet so delicious.
And there you are gorgeous and valuable and
acquiescent and whole whose feet stand you up,
and smile snaps you level, and hope pulls your
great frightened mass of aliveness through the world,
and fear shoves you back, and obstinacy leans
you forward into the claws of the wind, and
beauty sears your eyes into the fire of desire
("Holy shit!" he mutters about a stunner in
his vision), and grief sits you down on your ass
like a boulder, and jubilation flings your blood
into the circles of the air, and greed grabs need
and rips out throats, and joy electrifies toes
into dance, and rage explodes your breast
like a mushroom cloud in reverse, and agape´
flattens you into an inner-planetary hug, and lust
returns you into a bullet splitting air,
and tenderness hurls you over-the-falls,
and love,love,love alternately reconstructs you
stronger and cracks your bones one by one--
the cartilage in your nose, the match
sticks of your fingers and toes, the bell house
of your skull, the chalk of your thigh bones,
the brittle timber of your ribs, and packed sand
of your hips--all crushed like a ruby-throated
thrush under the enormous closing pressure
of the valentine fist. So go easy, be kind
to the oozing baklava, the popover, the puff-
pastry stuffed with blueberry, blackberry, almond,
or pecan; the spinach and feta strudel
wrapped in buttered gauze; the deep-dish
pie steaming from the oven, bubbling, tantalizing,
gold around the edges with a yielding heart...

Gently, but authoritatively,
he swipes her with the blunt arc of his paw,
gurgles, then rolls onto her,
his mane tumbling to one side, like wheat.
She growls, pushes him as if away
with only one surge of her boundless will,
then opens to admit his vibrating bridge,
which he lowers into her, like a wish,
and, in honest witness of the sun,
the Baobab trees and the nation of cranes,
in the cradle of the sweet-grass,
the ticking bugs, and the shooting fronds,
in the center of a golden field,
their fur softened in the heat, like beds,
they free the beams inside their breasts
through slits they rip with passion-claws
in each other's skin. The bright rays flow,
the blood-red rush of evening's flood
slammed off their living walls and
shot into the stars, until, spent, they
lie splayed, like calla lilies, leg-petals
fallen open, on their backs, mouths
slack, dozing in the dying sun. Human
beings, muscled, belligerent, elemental,
arms and chest capable of applying
an enormous number of pounds of pressure
per square inch, territorial, and dense--
tendons extending to the ends of their fingers
powering the grip--
don't try to come between one and his mate.
It would be to stick one's hand in a mill.
Even the most meek, upon feeling piqued,
finds his thumb in a fist or his fore-finger
on the eyelash trigger of a gun.
What happens when a woman splits her thighs
to let her man in, climbs up his balls,
is something more than nerves and flesh,
or the ignition of hot blood.

I see it with peripheral vision in your feet
in the rush of copulation--
strong, blunt, underestimated, ecstatically
arched, stiff, V-ing toward the sky
as if you were pulling some primitive law
through the sap of your toes: the statute
of ownership and the interlock of knowledge.
We know each other, and therein
form beliefs. We, all of us, are so
adorable: the furniture of the eyes
(brows, lashes, curves), the tenderness
of the lips, the sweet groove along
the contour of the spine, nipples
and aureoles, the rounded curves
of the sex, the soft halos of hair,
the beauty of the Achilles phrase
tapering to the slender heel,
but just beneath the surface
of the skin, like an inserted metal plate,
lies the hard muscle, the tight net
of selfishness, jealousy, desire,
the fear of hollowness, in-
satiability, hunger, pride, the howling
for completion, greed, insecurity,
possessiveness, the need to nurture,
the need to fold in, knowledge,
knowledge, knowledge which once inhaled
creates us.
It is playful, but deadly serious,
the having of a mate,
and the males have very sharp knuckles.

I roll off her, satisfied, fired, heart
cutting back to its resting pace, and
think of my father and the words he
spoke in his separate bedroom about
my mother, "We're finished." I
breathe the air of satiation and remember
the interminable war of my parents'
marriage, fists and spittle flying
through rages, children crying. I
yearn for peace with the legacy of war
foaming my blood. I close my eyes and clutch
the woman who has just tossed me wildly
into my skin, and see the visages of two
combatants defending themselves, slanting
forward, discolored, veins popping.
"You're worth more dead than alive,"
one screams, and the other retorts,
"Go to Hell," my sister and I driven
to our rooms, feeling blamed. I
stroke my lover--speckled, pliant, firm,
risen--in the grainy dark and roll
in the low, sweet tones of her velvet
voice. I subdue the impulse to demand,
"Mother, beat me, rip me for this
murderous retaliation," believing all
love conceals vengeance in its paws.
Now, half dead, my mother a tumbler
for tears, my father Valium soused,
sharing little more than the same
brick walls, I admit that I cannot
rescue them, not with my multiplicity
of song, not with my profession, not
by pulling off a coup de grace.
I lay beside the fragrant field of
the woman I adore, eyes shut, shoulders
folded into themselves, like the blunt
wings of a bird of prey, and hear through
the howl of my torrents of blood a thin
voice cry, "There's breath in
the onrush of death. Valiant boy,
in the terror of this love, kill
them, save yourself, save yourself."

Levolor blinds closed behind the extravagant
fern, we cuddle, arm in arm, legs overlapped,
mouth-to-mouth. Skin tingles and tongues
intertwine, like the double streams of a Venician
fountain. Love subdues into apathy. The
rainforests burn while we ignite each other.
Down of your back yields to my hairless palms
as the hardwoods fall. Two snails, our mouths
confuse their lives into one another, soft-rimmed
caves. Hear the roar of extinction in rich soil
as the bedsheets hum. My blood leaps to
flow through yours, red into red, skin
peeled back, like eroticized plums, exposing
engorged lush flesh. Who are we? Bones in nerves,
marrow in bones, tender, bewildered, honest, alive,
holding each other, like a breadmaker's fold.
I slide my penis into you and the whole world
dims--cormorants soaked black with Exxon
on Alaskan shores, the shredded child, run-
away plumes of gritty smoke in the Persian
Gulf, the crumbling gods, the seizure machines,
blood red dawns. Ecstasy softens us. Sweet...
kind....I am afire with you, dance
behind my flaming eyes, throw my blood.
Romantic love recycles cans and defuses hate.
Stroke me, smear me, be Cleopatra to my jungle
cat, legs fallen open, behind our blinds,
in soft coolness, apart from the complicated
destruction of the world. Come into me,
like a newborn's crown. I am so weary of human
brutalities: the faithless woman who combines
the semen of two men in her sour laboratory
of flesh, the humiliation of sons, the daddy
exciting his daughter's vagina, and--deepening
the sum--the asphyxiation of fetus Earth,
the splitting of her placenta, the straight-pinning
of her eyes, the mutilation of her vulva,
bombardiers in roaring swords blistering

her air. Love dulls an edge while
bracing the nerves. We cover each other
in buttermilk folds, stroll, break the sun
around our bones, bite down on pride, expose,
expose, and, running down the blunting slide,
make love beneath the ozone hole in hot winter.

Afterward, he wondered about the enormous and complex
connectedness, the intertwining of tendrils delving
deep into the ground, the DNA spiral of love and histories
plunging into dark loam their inextricable root systems
of dependencies and desires. He thought of the apparent
simplicity of cows, sweet, brown-and-white spotted Holsteins
who mount each other in open fields, multiply, and low;
who shake their necks and wander off into valleys
stupid and indifferent. He stared at his chock full
bookshelves, the multi-colored spines of novels and non-
fiction, the encyclopedias and dictionaries, the OED, the tome
titled, "Dissection of the Vertebrates," and wanted to hide.
The blinds rattled from a mountain breeze as he lay
with her--cactus needle, aspen leaf, and cottonwood spume
fragrances filling their dusk-rich room. How huge, he pondered,
are our heads, like great glass globes scrimshawed with
complex geographies and delicate intricacies. They bang
against one another on ordinary strolls through public streets,
cracking at times, like fault lines. Pride straining
the faint capacity of weak necks. Afterward, he gloried
in the rich confusion of being human, the intermixtures
of love and reticence, the textured knowledges, the almost
infinite possibilities. His eyes rolled, like sparkling
marbles, wobbling to the source. He felt so blessed he wanted to
prick his finger to see the dark blood. He wanted to suck
his toes to feel the pillow tongue. "Contours," he thought,
the word "contours," "curves," "sensuality," "bones," "tendons,"
"knees," "words." The unfathomable alphabet of longing, the
refusal to stop wanting. This is life. Wanting is life. His
penis felt cold surrounded by air, by the room, the breeze
drawing across it, like water. He thought of the agony of his parents
in Texas, in Corpus Christi-- "Body of Christ." How his father,
paranoid, guilty, and ashamed bruised his mother, knocked her
to the cold bathroom floor; how he pops his pills. So beautiful
and tragic. He felt like a fish quivering on a hook. He
thought of beautiful diners at outdoor cafes, under the shadow
of mountains, sipping coffees, flicking sandaled toes, and
speculating on the attributes of future lovers. How gentle
the bed sheets felt on his face--floral and new--as he lay

with his palm tucked under her thigh and his toenails brushing her
foot bones. What landslides fall within the skin, what acts
of confusion. Clear, his love for her, unquestionable--that is
not the issue--but life, like rock, pulls down. "What did you say?" he
blurted, but she had said nothing. He thought that if he
could retrace his life back to the fork, back through
the tree-and-leaf-crowded path to the critical point,
and progress anew...but that would be false and suicidal.
He would lose the one woman he loves. How packed hard
the earth is. "Oh," he thought, "what a plethora." Where
are the cows lumbering on simple femurs to the lovely slaughter?
He looked at his watch and it was 7:15. Afterward, he felt
the dark dilation that normally accompanies him, the flooding largeness,
the pool of ecstasy and blurred boundaries. Populations of
women and men bled into his pores, like trickling fords,
like finger lakes, and settled in his heart, as he bled
through them. Lost borders. Stretched head. Melted. But
focused, too, and sharp as steel. The contradictions. The
conundrums. If skin had pockets he could have slid notes in
to calm himself after the water rushed away. The baby wriggling
in its crib. The mother's throat. The easy sleep. Afterward...
after what?...fusion?...union?...coitus? After breaking apart
he thought of the swerve on ice, the soundless slide,
life turning sidewise on its axis. He thought not about
loss of control but the inexorable fact of motion. And once again
cows appeared in his dreams--heavy, docile, dumb, and,--
oh, what does he know of cow, cow love, cow sadness, cow joy,
cow complexity? They lumber head down, chests sagging, bones
sticking out, like scaffolding, burdened perhaps with the failure
of the world. Dispel this myth, man, of omniscience. All
he knows is that he loves the woman, that she fills him, that
he's loved by her, that he was born sticky and wild through
his mother's loins, that life seems like a black-ice skid
sometimes when he shuts his eyes. All he knows is what's
in the declension. Afterward, all his variables in unison sang
of the clear, hard realities: the lamp, the desk, the
chair, the bath tub, time's fine blows on the sun-thickened
window sill. Of those he sang,
and of life's spectacular uncertainties.

I want to pour children, like a pitcher of water,
through the hallways of my company: waifs, urchins,
gamins, orphans, brats, prima donnas, toddlers in
diapers, darlings of the upper-class; to roll them outward,
like a basket of eggs, from which individually
they would burst, whole and adorable. What a
mountain breeze that would be. What an exhalation.
To see them shrieking through the halls: the bow-legged
babies, the mischievous grade-schoolers, the lawless
pre-adolescents hole-punching the memo pads, defacing
the fax machine, dancing with in-boxes on their heads.
Primitive energy in this stale old hospital, like
the pulse of jungle drums. There in Matthew's office
Frederick pounds dumpling fists, wads Scotch
tape, coos fresh policy from his pouch of sweet
breath, and poops the Presidential chair. And little Prudence
dirt-smeared, diminutive, and dictatorial pontificates
from Peter's piles. From outside our structure would
appear a bastion of nationalistic pride, but inside
Justin would be yanking Debbie's hair, Chloe dumping
client files, and a barnyard of pigs, chickens, goats,
and hogs frolicking on the plain. Yes, I want to
reconstitute my office because I am sick of this
stiff-back sitting, this wrecking of spontaneity,
this snuffing of the soul. We were elected to be
their mentors, not their subduers. Let them miss the
urinals by a country mile, let them glop the rubber
cement. It's not a matter of disrespect, but of
keeping unpetrified. And I'm not an insurrectionist.
I want to loose a puddle of children from my palms, like
a genie who's scooped fertile mud: an ooze of hearts
jumping, a tadpole-like whipping through the
meticulous rooms. Sharpen pencils to the nub, bawl
for mother in a blast of honesty. We have failed
with our bright red pop cans, our cell phones,
our steroidial meat. We have served up hell in the
guise of success. Are you ashamed or is your pride
too steep? Have you been so inculcated that you can't

find the seams? Did you father's fist seal your brain,
and your mother's screams? Can you rebuild the citadel?
I want to release them, like a spasm of sea lice,
en masse, agglomerated, bricked-together, who are
abandoned by divorce, dragged screaming by the wrists,
criticized, beaten, taught lessons, sexually abused,
exploited, desolidified, in horrible times flipped in
the air, caught on saber blades, and occasionally loved;
to see them burst through the doors, explode into joy,
bubble the atmosphere, oh, seed the labyrinths! Until then
I will ache for the crack in the core which lets them in.

And there I am on a rubber raft, saltwater
washing through my mouth, giggling at seven
in the knowledge of parents: a father
with coarse, black hair and a mother like a crow,
strong with flight feathers. Jewish boy
on the beach, pail and shovel, drenching sun,
roar of the surf, Portuguese men-of-war
washed on shore, like marbled dirigibles,
and strong fishermen guiding my life through
the variables--Irving with dark speckles,
Shep with boulder thighs, Harold no less
influential for his florid skin and feminine
side which wedged through him, like a fin. It was
jubilance and resonance and sand grit and
gutted trout and sexy wives with lacquered nails
who bitched and loved and donated and slathered
their dumb children with Solarcain. Women
with that kind of leg skin which exudes
sexuality: smooth, freckled, white, pliable,
like the underside of fish. And their children,
little vessels of innocence filled with
immortality and egoism bucking in the sun-pound.
It was Rome before the fall, solid curves of
toughness in the parents like walls, gold
flowing through scotch and blended whiskey
necks, and Texas Longhorn football bursting
like concussion bombs. Nothing crumbled no matter
how brittle it became because there were money,
guts, kids, wives, glory, and the whole great
God damned Gulf of Mexico glittering with gamefish.
And there I am floating on my rubber raft
where the ocean floods the shore, laughing,
breast full of glee, stuffed like a turkey
with sweetness and deflected rage, no
more the carrier of the clear blue flame
of poetry than the carrier of bubonic plague.
It was that textured storm in the brain,
blurry happiness which thrives and throws

off sparks of luxury in the veins. It was
fish-scaling knives and bellowing men
and Port Aransas, Texas, and God's diamond
jewelry broken and spilled over the horizon,
like a sea. It was semen and fertility
and seed flung in the flesh of wives,
like meteor showers in the infinite sky.
And children folded into the prayer of two hands
before bedtime in the hearing of seawaves,
sailed into their dreams, like schooners,
flawless and streaming with praise.

See me slice down the face of a wave, like
paring knife and potato, strips and curlicues
stiffening, then raining across the tube; a
thundergod. This is no metaphor. I am surfing
Port Aransas, Texas, on Sunday, wetsuited,
February, cold offshore breeze. A rare jewel
of a day in what is usually split pea soup.
Doesn't a teenage boy have the right to a little
fun without a parent chasing him, like a pig?
The waves feel powerful, like Behemoth humps
rising out a floor and rolling forward in rage.
Do you know how freeing it feels to control such
power? My "friend," that anti-Semitic thug,
freaked on weed, drowned here last summer,
choking, like a cat. Good for the Jewish sea!
Over my back the horizon rises into a bowl
of blue sky, nothing but seamless shades
of azure, cerulean, blue-green, baby blue,
sapphire, aquamarine, and crystal beads of water
blurring my eyes. The immensity out there.
I sit on the continent of my WeberPerformer,
Rodin's "The Thinker" with legs immersed in
water, flunking school. I'm nothing for books.
See my Jams and black skin flash against the sun,
myself a fin on a finned thing. What it would be
like, I wonder, to slip it to a girl
at night on a sand dune; to slip it
to Sheri Long, for instance, that dripping
babe, or Dianne Wyneken? Watch me carve
this wave. No, no. It's just a serpent
sliding under me. This one, then. Oops,
another snake. A sea-vat of snakes. Let one
raise its cobra-head and I'll show you how
to ride it down its cold belly to the tail,
and kick out before it kills. That's
what I can do. Oh, to fuck Dianne Wyneken.
Oh, my gonads! What a bodily lurch to be
alive, sproutings everywhere, like a thorn

tree. I want to slice open my breast
and sing. I sometimes imagine the bleeding
crimson line as I razor down the center
of my chest, pull apart the walls, and
release what's there--a flock of birds and
dicks. I'm all feel. Blue are my hands,
blue my lips. Let's bring it in on one
last big wave, like the one on the album cover
monstrous and feathering, and probably roaring,
like a firestorm. Yes! Yes! Here it comes!
Free. Free. The prison door trembles
to fling open, at last.

And when I pulled a ribbon fish from the depths--
my God, it looked like a lethal umbilicus--
my father shrieked, "Look out, a shitsky!"
and he ripped the rod from my wrist so I would not get
sliced by its teeth. It shimmied and flicked,
brilliant snake, like a strip of razor wire,
flinging blood and silvery waterdrops everywhere.
But the pliers came, needle-nose, and down crushed
the foot over its flattened length, and my father
ripped out its guts with the treble hook and flung
it back into the blue-green deep. Stunning beast,
primeval, head full of teeth, instinctively darted
down like a sunbeam, before dying. On the deck
its blue-red throat, slime, clots of gore, a slash mark
were all that remained. The boat rocked in the sloughs,
like a cradle, and a pelican stared indifferent as a rock
as the clouds sailed by. And then later under the hammer
sky, I shrimped my hook, waited, my lips parched and
un-soda-popped (we drank them dry), my baseball cap shielding
my Jew eyes, I hauled up a dogfish, spiny, dangerous,
useless, tough; it bloated, croaked, dared me to touch
its urchin spines. He came again, this time gloved,
ripped the pole from my hands and, grabbing the line
three feet above the fish, like a sling with a stone
tied to the end, bashed it against the side of the boat.
Swung and bashed, swung and bashed, the dark weight
hooked in the throat-bones hanging on to this hellish
ride. But soon its tail began to explode, like plastic
strips, flying apart, pieces spiraling through
the air, gray and pink, sticking in its own black
blood to the prow, and then, its sides frayed and
split, spikes and needles spewing outward, like exploding glass,
its body slammed into a pulp, until finally it slid off
the hook into the grave of its birthplace. All that
remained of this Shylock fish: blast marks, black spots,
whip burns, where it hit and hit the side of our
ship. I stood like a king in the Colosseum
and watched. Sea wind parted my locks, sea gulls

swooped, and little pools of water soaked
my feet. It's not profound to say the great ocean
swallows its dead, like a mother, sealing the
wounds they make sliding in. After the pink and blue
ripple, the violence, the splatter of guts, a mirror
closed over the wound and the back-sloughs shone,
quiet as glitter. There is a craft skimming over
cold water, an Evinrude, pieces of raw flesh and
cutbait, an aerator sparse with shrimp bits, tackle
boxes, rods, reels, bloody hands, gaff and fish net,
boatsides nicked and cut, curved, like swan wings,
and a boy and his dad gliding over radiance toward home.

Oh Popsy-baby, let me have myself straight from the
palm-open of your heart, delivered like a pearl on
an oyster tongue, let me have my surfer hair to flip
sidewise like a cock-butt, let me have my indolence--
I'm 13 big ones and an individualist. Don't flush
the toilet on my head. Oh Daddyboy give me my blood
sticky & red to fling into my flesh like a string,
my blood-your blood without unleashing that red scream,
"Grow Up!" Daddyhead stop working so much and catch
my ball screwily flung into your mitt. What's so great
about a cigarette machine in a beer joint, that cold
green steel and quarter spill, filthy, slick? The
little money sack? Oh Daddyfuck put your bristly
mouth-beard over my snail-lips and give me mouth-to-mouth
in the parking lot, my head slunk back 'cause I'm yer
come mixed with mumby-egg. Draw me a map, let me
scrap with a handful of dollarfilth and a rustbike,
free like an emancipite in the seawind, hair blowing
in a whipfest and tan laying on, 'cause you don't care
if your boy's himself in his sandy blown town, with
An Attitude, you've applied artificial resuscitation
and his lungs 'r pumpin' in his cellophane membrane,
you bet cher life, your son by God full of Bar Mitzvah,
hamantaschen, and himself. Oh daddybum don't blow
brains out like yuv yapped about off & on again, rather
lunge and tackle me shoulderpadded with the tucked
in pig. I'm going fast, like a tinderfire
enveloped in ageflame: acne, facehair, full bush,
headed for goneness but for a burnmark on the
pinefloor. See the firepit of my loins. See
my branches flame. Then I'll be the lotus opener
and you'll be petrified in rage, old prunepit, canyon-
pile, dungstone. Old fathermine. Don't do it.
Don't pop those cockpills all night in their pill bins,
so coffinesque--diazepam & sleep hammer--nor cuddle
EST like a shock-junkie, no, go, for me, into the scare
house on the hill of your psyche, find the killers,
cry, shatter teeth, fling on the lights and make them
fly--bats--cloud of fears into the sun-strike bleeding
dry and white, so that you & I might, Daddypot & boy-
tyke, dance our feet stinging on this dazzling rind. Please.

In the penis colony the men lounge in overstuffed
chairs near the hot buffet talking statistics
and percentages. The ceiling cathedrals and
the sounds are carpeted. Pipes of pin-stripes
stove their legs, socked and gartered in Bergdorf's,
and a signet ring corsets every third piggy. In
the penis colony the chef stuffs an apple between
guilt's snout, bakes it pink and blade-succulent, and
serves it in a glaze of shame sauce. All goes down
easy through the gullet of rage. "What say we have
a game," one suggests, all cheer, the mansion rocks,
and they pull out a gorgeous one from the stock
room: sexy-wet, fresh, full blush, cotton blouse,
untouched, adorable. Her little lungs heave.
"A blonde!" one looking like Mr. Monopoly Tycoon
shouts, and in a swarm the sport ensues. One
tenderly, upon his knees, proposes matrimony, hee!
hee! hee!, another lays down, as if over mud, his
glistening coat, deeply bows, and another pours
her a pink champagne while the face-blacked one
posing as the butler bolts the door. Then, one
plucks at her: a hair, a brow, a titty-tit-tit,
and getting very hot, all chime in. A welt of blood
back-floods and surges through the stump as one rips
off her apricot ear, three or four firmly plant
shoes and tear out an arm--have you ever seen
that gristle and bone rainbow in the baked chicken
leg?--and fall to, eating, one gouges out a gold-
flecked eye and pops it, like an egg, and several
wishing on a side, split her in two by the legs.
And the ritual begins: out come the knives. The
President gets the liver, the Vice President the
spleen, the Treasurer the bladder, the Secretary
her pancreas, the Sergeant-At-Arms both kidneys, and
to the members, the loyal members go the intestines
(both king and queen), the uterus, the pancreas,
the fallopian tubes, the eggs, the bladder, the sails
of the lungs, the brain, the lips, the slab of the

tongue, the esophagus, and all the scraps, a feast
beyond the believable, while outside under the
sweltering glow, along the skeleton of the city,
glide the oblivious commuters in glossy steel
bubbles. Afterward they scrape clean the
counter. Her heart they throw to Fi-Fi the poodle.

I've taken flight like a flashing colorbird,
quick-winged, darting for the greening foothills,
over the speartops and the greenblades, whirring
like some kind of tissue machine, sweetly
into the Blue-Blue; scarlet-streaked, emerald-
swathed, golden-topped I am; Tinkerbellbird
hovering into the honey tube, beak-dipping,
streaking for red trumpets, and climbing, fruit-
fueled--cantaloupe, nectarine, blackberry,
apricot--light-like, flitting on slumberjoy,
flush with iridescence. Within my atmosphere swirl
the computer, the MasterCard bill, the antiseptic
tube, Fresca and her contemporaries, and the
shrapnel shell turning nebula-esque about
my chest--hefty things stuffed with wheels
& gears, which I, birdily, could scarcely lift. Mama
stardusts up with me, like a wake, Daddy sparkles,
and babies Milky Way as I flash & flit--birdboy,
hummerman. You'll know I've been through by
the trembling bluebells, the shivering feeders,
and the bulleted aspen leaves. No waxwinged
Icarus--dilettante!, experimental boy!--woozy with
arrogance elevatored to his dripdrip, I hover, spin,
wheel, catapult backward (split-tailed), bow, and
burrow into the honeypile, like the court jester
booming on rocket fuel--now that I couldn't care
less, now that life's nowhere, now that earth's
exposed itself as a helmetful of...HA!...now that
I know The Secret--which I'm not revealing--though
it involves the fact that Dreams mean nothing,
money is immaterial, science is a bit of flat-
ulence, the family is a cup of fog, and your
favorite tree--the one spray-painted green upon
your brain--isn't. I wrap my arms around "so what,
big deal" like a hippo-big soap bubble, and
suddenly I'm shooting nimbus-ward, skydrilling,
midair halting, tail feathers ashovel. Slim Pickens
slapped the sides of The Bomb with his hat as

he rode it down, his life gone mad--a symbol of
The Recognition--and I roll, soul-blown, free
of relevance, fuck it all--it's okay, it's
unbelievably fine, it's not important anymore,
or even real--nevermind what--we all abandon Daddy
in our own way--bye-bye. And this particular
day I'm vibra-happy, punch-silly, and ecto-stunning,
and I'm borne on air, effortlessly, in full skeleton.

If I could stick my tongue through the fat portion
of my palm, completely through so that it waggles on
the other side, like a worm or a soft sword; there
I would find God: an ordinary tongue, an ordinary
hand, but an extraordinary moment--a tongue penetrating
the soft lips of a hand which water-close around it
when withdrawn. God would be there--I am certain--
where the flesh gave way to the wetness, where the
little opening parted for the rooting tip, magically.
This fertile garden in the palm of a hand is where
the true sanctuaries on earth reside; where priest,
deity, and prayer converge in one act of privacy. The
tongue is sweet, like an apricot; the hand salty,
like a sea; and the tissue and blood within the hand
are thick, sticky and pushing, like a wall. I think
of joists and hinges, bolts and headnuts, but here
there is no grinding, gouging, nor dust of saw. It
is almost sex. There are sacred places--grottoes--
where self collides with self sans robes and hymnals--
where the red mouth of a dog breathes in dusk, and
the jewel of a wildcat's eye flares. Try it in your
tattered clothes, in your destitution-cell, with ash
smeared on elbows, and love gone mad. If I could
stick my tongue through the fat of my hand--there's
a blue crab clamped to my heart, a blue crab is
clamped to my heart, something leapt on me at birth
which was blue and hard and it clamped to my heart,
my heart wears the lid of a blue crab shell, the
first three beings I laid eyes on were my mother, my
father, and a broad blue crab--if I could stick my
tongue through the fat of my hand, like a sun-
slash through sky, without anyone noticing, in the
solitude of my room, God would appear, like a sea
floor after the moon draws up the gown into its
globe. There's a knife and there's the robe and
there's the secret soon beneath the robe. The hand
splits and the palm becomes lips, eye, vagina, and
the entering tongue self-love flooding. We all
crumble a little inside. If I--if you--could pass
material through itself, your fists might unrage,
letting milk pour in. Raise your hand to your lips,
finesse your tongue, in your mind slide it through.

You think the walls will fall down and you
will flood through the rooms of love--if you
just meet the right girl--foaming and swirling
forward in your masculinity over the downed
barriers; and the girl--you have an image of
her in your head: a shoulder-length pixie-cut
black haired blonde, buxom with tiny breasts,
toweringly small. You know she exists, like
that legendary Palomino in the hills you're
yet to sight. You come home nights to your
flawed compromise mated before the falcon of
awareness angled into your blood melting you,
like nickel. You notice her pores and moles,
and the dullness of her eyes, and think of the
starved fire of yourself--and all around--at
work, at the club, at the coffee boutique you
identify replacements, perfect in some way you
want to possess. Oh, you're an eye-slit panther
on the boulders capable of slashing the dark-
ness bloody, and you're poised to leap. Your
downy under-hairs ruffle in the breeze. The
walls will fall down, like hurricaned homes,
and you will flood through with love, like
an angry tide--your sister doesn't know, your
mother doesn't know, your colleagues don't
know how dangerous you are, your head a
cauldron of hot, liquid gold, "Yes," you acquiesce,
"I'll do a memo on that." They don't know the
deep throbbing power your buttons hold back.
You'd like to kill them. If you opened your
overcoat all the women of the world would rush
in, as if sucked. Today God convinces you
you need a young girl--tart and round--to
scintillate, to pull you down through the
gauzy silver clouds, to mint the tarnished
plate of you, perpetually, and to chirp on the
flashing line, tail feathers shifting in the
wind. And there you are in the parlor of

your mind--Centaur man--with your shirt down,
torso tapered to a V, sipping from a fantasy
fiction pond, cantering across a wood, and
the sun showering needles, and the zinnias
bursting open, and the waft of crushed cran-
berries thick upon the air, and you nibbling
the foot-ridges of your slave-baby, like a king.

I pluck our baby from your womb and stick it
under the flap of my midriff. I, male, am pregnant!
I do what woman does. I nurture the child in my
ocean while its heart crashes against my palm. I
groan and eat and witness the upheavals as the
world rushes and recedes in significance. I steal
the babe and slip it in the mesa above my dick
under the hairswirl and abs in my little pocket
of significance. If you are bereft I am filled, no
longer a busker's happy balloons twisted into
a vapid dog. I have curves and globes and
The Bulge and the beautiful blue womb. I cry. I
flare with rage. I bathe in the sumptuous tub, my
soul free of the violence man wreaks upon man in the
abattoir of the world. I am thief, yes, and plunderer--
but I am cucumber and glycerin too. I let you--
pencil and artist's pad--sketch me plumped under
tapestried quilts. My feet are clean and young,
like yeast. How sick I am of motherfuckers, the
pile drivers breaking and crushing lives, the an-
nihilators, the snap-up-and-eaters, meathunger. I
slip our zygote under my gown and wait for the
nurturing impulse to strike my wrists and lar-
nyx. We are in bed, our feet like twins sticking
out at both ends. Peace flows from the half-light
into my nostrils. I am content. I am fulfilled. I
am terrified. I rip the waist of my pants to make
them fit, and my breasts grow tender. I snatch the
baby in my beak, nest-robber, and slip it in,
and this is an unforgivable violence, my last. I
see my amniotically dripping hand. I see my hate.
I see envy's tongue, retract, slaked. I see our room
opening, like a cube, emancipatorily. I see you
weep. I see pink tissues turn brown. I see you
crumple, like a soggy stick. I see darkness resmear
your face. I see the loss, an empty pocketbook. I
see the scream bubble your lips. I see my bigness
increase. Being human--soul and teeth--I am capable
of embracing rich dichotomies but being male, and
with my funneling flame, I deprive you of everything.

I like the feel of cutting fruit--the pine-like
crispness of an apple; the way juice from a Bosc
pear sluices along the knifeblade; the kiwi; ba-
nana; cassava; mango; or cutting across the bias
of an orange, like one shattering windows; the
way apricot rises and gives birth to cold steel--
I am an animal--the manipulation of the knife in
my fingers, the way the handle molds along my palm,
like a mouse or the materialization of my mother's
song. See the grapefruit rind split, like a cry,
and weep its milky tears in the slender flash and
divide fully its two round halves to the cutting
board; the watermelon; the fig with its bag of seeds.
I could kill. I could bare the beauty of human
flesh to the moonlight, liquid red swirled with
silver light, white of bone shot with hues. What
kind of monster might I be? The grape peel bursts
and yields its filament veins to air, delicate,
green flesh clean as amniotica. And the
explosions of taste, human milk shot through
nipples into the mouths of babes, their heads
receiving, pliable little legs dangling off cliffs
of air. I love the feel of cutting fruit, like
fingerblood, plum red, oozing through an accident.
There are the broken bodies of men and women lac-
erated in steel cages, bleeding beautifully, bodies
hanging, like slaughtered beef. There are the
opal bruises and the black eyes which are truly
rainbow blue and green tinged with god, and ir-
idescent. There are the colors of danger and
disaster and ultimate demise. --The juices arc
onto Veteran's Day lawns, thick and green, as
The Spangled Banner outwardly spills. We are
imperilled by our disease of wounds and wounding.
There! The tomato pours forth a flood, like a
mother, Mother, when they wheeled you to the ICU
bearing four fat heart-sunk tubes, you were sluic-
ing blood, fine long threads which looped in air

and recirculated back through a leg, and I was
your little boy again in sun-parched shoes crying,
"mama, mama," --human fruit, both of us. The ac-
cident plows. We look up. We have broad chests.
The father waits. The mother knows. The children
sing. The baby rests. Under my hand, along the
knife blade, the fruit of the world trembles and
gushes forth its seeds and meat and sugars and hair
and pools and sheets and pattern and core, a plenti-
ful shell--a precious cave--which empties beautifully
and thickens my fingers, like a necessary disaster.

Mother devours her sons through the mouth of
her vagina, like steak. She masticates, lu-
bricates, swallows them in meaty lumps, and
jams them back in--fetuses--rehooked to
the chord, like astronauts to their pumping
ship. The sons fight, flail in their envelope of
space, cling to their mates, like climbers to
cliffs, but always succumb to the monstrous
suck. It may take years. Mama's an ape, a hairy
beast, and a vacuum, and through her slit lies
a grotto of teeth. Boy smashes them with a
rock but they regenerate sharper and more a-
mazingly human. Son studies his hands, his feet,
the little brush strokes of arm hair, his tendons
and veins, and doesn't understand. Why can't I...?
How does she...? I'm no mullet but a suspension
bridge-of-a-man tough with cables and concrete
solid in the gusts. Mother craves him and undercuts
his legs--oh, he has located a woman to betroth,
chestnut and pink, alabaster and red, spiritual
and full--and powers to her up mountainous land,
but he slides back down Mother's avalanching
funnel into her gullet at the vortex snapping
off his future world his shocked lover's face and
flinging it into the firmament forever. Hear the
roar--inferno--engulf his arms, and the teeth threshing
and the punctured heart spouting rage. Hear
the crystal shatter, the keys melt in the mouth
of fire, and the anger well. "Mama! Mama!" the
man-boy yells, and hear the relief, yes, the relief
at the arrival of a strange familiarity, home.
--------------------mirror-----------------------------------
The boys intertwine their bodies and fly for home.
The peninsula of Florida is no less massive than their
missile. Their sides and nose cone split the air. No
jagged obstacles block their path, not calcium or quartz-
edges nor lipsticked women radiating love and yeast
and heart's blood. The rocket-boys, radar equipped,

blip on the screen, like an inexorable asteroid,
incoming, headed for ground zero, planet earth,
the bull's-eye: mama's bones. She may not want
them, may dodge like a criminal bathed in ultra-
red, or she may crave them, like a drug,
but flocking they fly back into her vintage wine,
and pull shut the cork. "Mama," they purr,
and curl like a warm wisp of smoke for the long
hibernation. They are shut down. They are on
life support. They have slipped into the thick-
walled aqualung. Here one hears no jarring sounds,
only mufflings, pillowings, and softenings,
and here one rides the pouch, a wallaby,
blowing raspberries at the sun. The sons flute
their gills, agoraphobic and horrified, great
avoiders of intimacy's vast land, virtuoso an-
nihilators of consummation, and re-virginize them-
selves white as veal. They bathe in mother's
juice and blood, her slippery chute, and grab
their feet and slide, "wee!," as the wind blows
their faces and their hearts rise and they tumble
all naked and clean and cherub-like in their non-
threatening paradise: graham crackers, milk, and
flannel jammies, all tucked in and her muscle shut,
and unanswered goes every knock upon their door.

419

Cut off the tip of my finger slicing turkey
the day before your heart surgery, mom, my
memorial to scalpels and blood. Took four months
to heal and even now it vibrates like an iron
bell. Mon and son, Jewish, hooked, a couple of
losers. The surgeon cracked you through, sewed
you up, now you're fine save for the two worms
crawling chest and thigh. Now, I've broken up
with my sweetie pie, my finger's fine, you're
paddling in the wading pool, the sun's banging,
and the sky's some cerulean eye scooping us
both, a shovel. No wife's going to rise in
bed--your prediction--and slaughter me with a
butcher knife, `cause there's no wife, `cept you,
mom, with your bristly beard. I give up. I masturbate
to your red toe nails. Not that I wanted you
to die in surgery, but a little liberation theology
from the grave wouldn't hurt--did you know, PS,
I was the only family member to cry. Besides,
you bleed money and I want mine. I'm forty-five.
Our lives are joined by their garbage--you've
got Dad and I've got you. You refuse to die.
Look at the little wooly lamb from behind,
so cute--the back of my head. Don't swing me
round for not even God understands my face.
Now, healed--my finger, your prolapsed valve--
the earth we walk upon burned clean, I search
the personals ads for a new baby: fit, blonde,
blue, looking for romance. Even monsters try.
How ugly this is oozing like pus from a brain.
I'm ashamed. But there it is. You have maybe
ten years and I about thirty-five and by god
geraniums in shut garages have done better. I
crush planets in my eyes. I'm glad you didn't
die and that Dad's, I hear, now holding your
hand (the guilt must be piled!), but I'm going to
stick the claw end of my hammer into my eye,
somehow, and remove you, like a nail, though it
be my last bursting, boiling, emancipatory piece
of effort this side of the God-blow. That's all.

It is the epoch of corporate inhumanity, officious shits
darting about office-places laying off people in the name
of efficiency, big corporations with knock-out logos
presided over by men. The eye glazes over. There are
ropy penises buried in the pouches of distant women
--all powerful appendages--octopus men driving hard
bargains; starvation in the guise of satisfaction--satis-
faction in the eyes of starvation. Dumpsters grow empty
while the anthropologists of garbage multiply--a greasy
wrapper, an old chicken bone. Blood in the veins flows
like lava, dignity or not, life's red rush feeds the brain
under skull's cap, hears from the boss, "Lousy luck...sorry...
had no choice." A gull dies in thick oil. There it is,
a perfect film: character, conflict, denouement. The
drain swirls down a person's life. I wretch home in
my hobbling car, another sorry story told, to the boy
of the dream shattered or gone, my abandoned offspring,
angry on guitar. It is a swell period, a humdinger, a
polished chrome time in the profit bowl, in the tech-
nology pit, digitals streaming across the eye, the
cyclopean screen switched on, like a screaming mouth
tight and wide. I want to pick up a piece of string, a
dirty warm thing, map of a past, drenched in child's
dry spittle, clutch it, roll it in my fingers, feel its
bumpy progress, savor the tiny history inscribed therein:
sensory, primal, basic as a sow grunting in mud or
clods flying from a horse's flight, jam it in my pocket,
like a piece of life unbroken by dehumanizing circuitry.
It is the epoch of betrayal, force-down decisions, karate
blows to the spine. Now it is time to chant, "All is
lost, all is nothing," at the terminal, at the work
station, at the virtual world, "All is lost, all is nothing,"
through the coffee steam, "All is beyond, all is over,"
like a flock of egrets gliding home, "All is--"
whatever word you wish to insert for devastation.
Time to give your heart's flesh to its eater, to shave your
head, to cup river water in your palms, time to abandon
control in the fragmentation. Time to lie in bed and

let the world devour you, like a cone. And so my
love, my no longer mine, I lie under the hail of our
flying apart, pieces of you hail and whistle down slicing
the tops of my ears and my thighs, and thickening the sky
like a cloud of birds. Under this I lie. I prepare to die,
and I die backward into the resurrection of the open hand.

My father and Irving, who would ultimately drown,
and "Uncle Shep," who wasn't my uncle--all three who
would be awake and casting by 5:00--snored sonorously
in their primitive beds side-by-side on the screened
porch of the "Mouse House" in Port Aransas, Texas,
on a hot summer night. They were men in undershirts
with wives and businesses and children and hair-whorls
turning gray toward middle life, men with salt-stiffened
sneakers and banged-up skin leaning toward red, God-
defying mortals beyond the mid-point. Snoring, as I
crept home with two black swollen eyes, two shiners
punched black by thugs on the beach within earshot
of The Music Machine by the pavilion's east-facing wall.
Unconscious and dragged into the surf by a friend to
waken me and off I slunk to the bed beside my dad, who
started at my arrival, but sunk back, an unnoticeable
sleep-hump. Sea towns are rough. Teenagers are mean.
What did I know of loathing in the soul and blood-lust
or the sheer cutting power of human knuckles? Next
morning a "buddy" kicked sand in my face and I still
admired him. The sea was diamonds, the waves were fine,
the warmth was motherly, but the water stung and no
matter how small an ocean seems, it's huge, which is
what Irving discovered one day with his life. I don't
remember what they caught or the legendary fish fry
or the following days at school skulking about the halls
with black eyes or my sister's surprise or my pain or
my classes or the cafeteria-shame or my girlfriend's
sympathies, just the first blunt blow to my face arriving
from nowhere and falling to the sand and covering
my face and being kicked and the word "Jew!" snapping
the air and the surf soaking my clothes. Nothing
more. A little brain tattoo. It wasn't the Holocaust, just
a little beating in Port Aransas of human flesh which
recovered and continued functioning, what you might call
a little insignificance. I found no solace in my parents,
but then who or what comforted them in their suffering?

Without consciously knowing it I depended on my Daddy
to go to work each morning and return each night with food
on the table. I came home from screwing up at school
each day--slouch, hot shot, practical flunkey with a smarmy
face--to pork chops or prime rib and peas or potatoes and
ice cream or tapioca pudding--I expected this as my
birthright and unspoken due. And he did: slipped on his
pants, uncardboarded his shirt, slurped coffee, two eggs,
toast and every day went to the office, some sleazy vending
machine affair full of weevils, machine guts, syrup bottles,
money filth, and steel furniture, King Daddy of the Milky
Ways. I can't imagine wasting life in such a hell, but, for the
yelling every night at mother, he seemed to love it, left each
morning, chest thrust, as if he were the heavy-weight
champion of the world, and, in fact, he was a pugilist. And
the corn boiled and the burgers fried and the ketchup ran
and the sundaes tickled and Daddy came and went day
after day, like a blurry shuffling of cards through a deck,
nothing but a whir in the air as he whispered by, and I ate
and ate, grew and wanted, and he was no god, but a brutal,
unanalyzed, repressed man medicated to the nines, but
I didn't care because I expected, like a butcher expecting
blade and block to cleave the neck, like a workman expecting
excavator and gasoline to move the earth, which is what, I
guess, life is: blood of the slaughtered sluicing in streams
and the earth puckering under gasoline. My daddy whom
I love but don't like was one of these finally nubbed to
family theft and common misery. And the other three
mantises of the clan--mother, daughter, I--by the fact of
our aliveness and constant need pitilessly watched him, a
perpetual motion machine, speed until he became a smoothed,
muttering piece of insanity. What did I care so long as
cells divided, flesh grew, brain multiplied, jaw clenched
on someone's butt--I had my furnace to feed and it raged
into sex and beer and drugs and cars and Burger Kings and
disregard and little pieces of attitude, peel outs on Saturday
nights, the jammed-open Holley burning the clutch into a fusion
of junk--daddy at work, daddy at home, daddy pumping down
pills with his head full of cheeping open-throated birds and the thud
of an ax blade meeting the block through an anonymous neck.

What was dinner time but a ship in a gale, the
table sliding fore-to-aft, the cables straining, the
liquids sloshing from cups, rocking side to side
and front to back, mother, father, daughter, son
the points of a cross over Formica, nightly, a gale
sending breakers to shatter the beams of the
ark, winds to rip down sails, swells....my father
caught me in mid-air leap across the table to knife
my sister, I saw her dead in my head, shouted
me down, and snatched the knife, my mother
snarled "more money" at my father who blew fire
into her hair, my sister shriveled into her shoulders,
like a scrawny bird, it was dinner in America
behind nice walls--meat, bread, butter, white
rice, Del Monte peas--unanalyzed, undivorced,
and unaborted; repression and her hostilities. My
grades were poor. I hated eggs. My mother
bitched. My father raged. I hated my sister. She
tortured me. The steak was tough. Too fucking
bad. Shut up or I'll give you something to cry
about. Go to hell. Monster! Bum! Dinner time and
the meal was us, we ate each other's livers out
when every White working male could afford a
strip of real estate and a body by Fisher, it was a
drum we made of the kitchen table whose reverberations
felt all night we shocked in motion by six o'clock.
It was a drum, an ark, a stage whose lights
clicked out, whose actors tattooed cigarette smoke
on boozy air, their makeup cracked; it was
the unintentional tragedy of blind optimism, the
middle dawn of TV--Sullivan, Caesar, Skelton,
Benny, California, Conoco--pumping into the family
brain primroses and promises it couldn't keep, it
was illusion outstripping reality across the
dinner table of the world compounded by the
usual human fragilities and the resultant dementia.
Yet, at my table one of us, at least, could split and
float above himself, a conscious balloon watching

the comical evisceration, mother, father, sister,
brother, braving the waves, securing the cups,
swallowing and forgiving, blaming and embracing,
who could see, bumping against the top left
corner of the room, the slow destruction of four
souls, the gradual erosion of joy or love or self-esteem,
or the just plain blessing of feeling right, and the
individual struggles in the boiling sea not to burble
under, and the occasional off-handed victories,
watching with his balloon face this happening to him,
too, while something unbreakable, immovable,
iron-solid inside cried, "but it is us, by God, it is us."

There might have been a hurricane and I might
have been in the waves straddling my Hobie
and waves might have hammered shedding spiny
spume and the waves might have sucked and
lumbered and the sky might have hemorrhaged and
the wind might have head-ripped and the rattlers might
have curled on roof-tops and the crabs might have
dug under and the men-of-war might have risen and
fallen on wild horses and the sting rays might have
saucered and my parents might have raged and
my parents might have screamed to me from
the cliffside beside the pink mansion and my parents
might have spewed acid and my parents might have
struck and the mullet might have submarined in gray
schools and the sky might have blotted and I might
have left white hand-prints in the sheen and I
might have hung up in the lip and I might have
dropped down the face of a gray elephant and I
might have stood on my world of foam and I might
have flown, flown and my parents might have
disowned and my parents might have died and a saw-
blade might have ripped my mother's stomach and
a knife blade might have slit my father's side and
there might have been a hurricane and I might have
been young and I might have snapped my Hobie under
my arm and driven it to the sea and I might have
straddled it in the wind-hammered gray dangling my legs
in a bowl of sharks and I might have drowned or
been devoured by any number of things and I might
have heard my father's voice straining into the
wind like a crooked-flying bird and I might have
heard and I might not have acquiesced but
paddled further into the mist where the elephants
herd and the zephyrs whistle in the delicate ear
bones and I might not have ever come back to the
solid brick house to the thick cool room to the neat
clipped grass to the clean round car to the rose red
mouth to the sparkling new curb and my father's voice
originating at the cliff might have plopped finally like a
stone in the sea a thousand feet short of my hearing.

As if my penis were are single piece of chromium steel
running from the base of my ass through my groin muscle
and flesh ten burning inches out into the deep, red dissolving
sun, one upcurved flaming shaft, I hammered her into the cotton
matting of the bed, full, then tickling thrusts about her lips,
male in female, locked, the pouring-in moon through parted
slats, two cravers quickened and thickened, then brought
back down to a water line, two clutchers forming one hip,
hole-squeezing-peninsula-filling-hole, the tight-fittedness
as I draw up and down across my inches stokes some
widely opening coal or bud, forcing me to keep going
all the way in all the way out so that her mouth, too, hungers
for the fire or flower to climb through us both, this is not
law nor the oath nor houses nor walls, but carnality in a crushed
down piece of field, blind, smelling of body and feces,
shameless, presenting and mounting, a melding of muscle,
bone, and mind into a single act of giving-greed, some Call
from lives just behind the door close to being made
appealing to power and dominance and the irresistible.
I--somewhere inside me a god claws, defying the frailty
of my nails--I prolong the pain of insatiable love--
triangles float above my brain, and thick red bars in the
semi-dark gold cove, and the bursting builds, my stomach
poufs above her curves in the open air, under which
I watch with blue intensity my penis appear and disappear,
like a Y and a V and a Y again, and I prop myself
up by my hands on her breasts, she is mine, all yielded,
unembarrassed--breasts, throat, toe nails, every inch outside
and in, thigh-flesh, tongue-tip, moat of eye, momentarily,
as am I, momentarily, all hers, not my mother's, not
my first nor second lover's, not revenge's nor shame's,
but hers, unique she with a name and a smell and a personality
and a mind, and all this coming and climaxing and slurping
and smelling and melting eyes and stage setting and
boundary loss and silk panties, all this mood-heightening
specialness and tenderness and fusion and "getting some"
and dispelling of the ghosts and transforming each other
alternately into permanent and unbudgeable mountains or

vibrating needles, all this squeezing the clay of each other's
flesh through the fingers, as if to sink in, cross through,
and trade bones, ganglia, images, pulses, and breath in one
ecstatic, unbelievable, comprehensive disappearing act is
secondary to this: the recognition across a crowded room
and the permission to take my place standing next to her.

511

I down the water hard, slam dunk it, really,
I'm in a hurry, skateboarding, sandlot ball,
little cellophane chest heart-heaving, little hands,
mother gaping--all my life I've been drinking
it, black rippled crystal in round glass, invisibly
saturating myself with its many psychedelic
permutations: Nehi, Coke, Jello, Popsicle,
lemonade, filling my cells, lining my bowels,
hydrating my eyes, and leaking it out me in
yellow arching streams through my urethra--
human fountain--collected it in plastic jugs as
Alaska's Fox Spring disgorged it up frozen
tubes, cupped and drank it from my palm raw
off mountain veins, boiled and cooled it in
the woods, from my own arms licked rain,
and of course the million spigots, fountains,
and hoses. Scientists say, in nineteen-ninety
six, that they are searching for life on Mars
by searching for water; the poles, they say;
the electrolytes that fuel the battery of life.
Such dependency begs a torture--subjugate an
enemy by depriving water, control the water,
poison the water, provide only enough water
to keep them begging, destroy with water--
rubies for the haves and ashes for the nots, such
a tidy box. And it burbles from the ground
and sheets down air's windowpane--aquifers,
lightning, limestone, manna clouds--and we
aerate it and chlorinate it and defilthify it in
unimaginable processing plants nestled between
foothills or flat along highways blooming water
flowers or stretching alongside outskirting
rye fields for the billion billion mouths and
biological systems to imbibe, suck, and knock
down endlessly without God, mind, light or
eye--its consummate invisibility--like love or
parents or family or friends which evaporate in
the blazing sun or torture of unconsciousness.

Fucking the Virgin Mary: she's my greatest conquest:
for her I am tender and wonderfully seductive--sincere,
boyish, open, and terminally listening, letting my
doe eye lashes work magic, convincing her that I am
harmless by playing the sensitive poet, psychoanalyzed
and enlightened. I tell her that I above all understand,
and sliding my hand over hers, that her deepest fears
are safe with me. No cheap Courvouisier seduction, I
move systematically into her soul or rather convince
her to open its door to let me curl there by playing
the sufferer, the youth abused by a brutal dad into a
wound requiring salve. This is achieved without
words, without hammer or nail, I employ her superior
intuition. She could never know that her cunt lies in
my cross-hairs, undulating, preparing to let me in,
partly because I repress from myself the full extent of
my dishonesty--the self-deceived is the finest
criminal. You would think that she would be clothed
in fluted white, but here on my couch she is wearing
muted red with black pumps and her leg skin is
creamy brown. I love her. I crave to slide my penis
between her breasts, such firm, heavy breasts. God
convinced her eternity exists on a shaft of air,
frictionless in a sea of emptiness, that the most
powerful man on earth sprung from the unbesmirched
womb. I have a bridge in London to sell! My gift
is pleasure, ecstasy, messiness, fluids, sucking, biting,
life's vicissitudes, connectedness, imperfection. I
acknowledge ego. Now I slip my hand under her
dress, now I feel her hair's wiry-ness, now she leans
down to kiss, now I glide one finger in, now her
tongue thickly comes, now a shoulder strap falls
down, now her bra is undone, now I tip one breast
from underneath, now she repositions herself on my
inexhaustible couch for my mouth, now I fasten, now
my pants are down and some flood surges against
thick tall walls within hearing, now her eyes are closed,
she breaks, and "gentle" quivers across my lobe, now--
you know the indescribable, miraculous slipperiness of
teenage lubricants, they net down the inner thighs and
can guide even the most oblivious in--now the blood
shatters under her broken skin. Oh Mary, Mary.

I tell the stranger sitting beside me on the plane which is
slanting in for a landing that I am going to rescue my
son from a psychiatric ward where his mother placed
him for experimenting with drugs and truancy, and the
stranger, a young woman, Born-Again, says, grasping my
hand and pressing her forehead against my arm, "May I
pray for him?" and proceeds to chant a most beautiful
prayer. She prayed as passengers filed by our side and
deplaned. The craft landed eventlessly and the visit with
my son was gut-wrenching and difficult. I brought him
home with me and, amazingly, he still lives! What we
cannot measure well we deify; Jesus is an immeasurable
commodity. My friend, long inexplicably depressed--
self-critical internal monologist, self-hating--worships
the serotonin reuptake pharmaceutical Zoloft, restores
balance daily, like a bath, to the immeasurable chemistry
of his brain. The twenty-four-hour-long self-regenerating
monologist dies, he says, at sunrise by the Marshall in the
pill--fast, deadly shooter. "I'll be on it for the rest of my
life," he adds. The great mysteries, the ones that over-awe--
Michelangelo's Chapel, *Les Miserables*, the Pyramids, the
microscopic gaps between human synapses: caverns we
fill with God to the brim, and over. How wonderful to
have glue to hold the whole together, clear, amber glue--
like bread--good, heavy bread to paste inside hunger.

541

So I'm watching Oprah interviewing teenage sex addicts--
we called them "nymphos" years ago--and their mothers--
and there's crying, accusation, hostile body language,
the works--all the daughters are beautiful, stacked, nicely
nosed, slender, and craved male attention, and admitted to
exhibitionist sex, adulterous sex, group sex, interracial
sex, monogamous sex, drug sex, and sex on the Internet.
None of them took money for it. One, looking into her
mother's eyes, said she could hook her father into fucking
her if she wanted, that he had made overtures. Oprah
was shocked. She spoke morality, birth control, re-
sponsibility, consequences, besmirchment, regret, ruination.
The girls sat unmoved. Then there were ads for Downy,
Advil, Tums, and Folgers. I peddled on my recumbent
Lifecycle machine contributing my whir to the whole,
humming club. Oprah, concerned for the fragile structure
of the universe, continued, the TV bolted to the upper
right hand corner of the room beside the fan, both tilted
toward the clientele. All that innocent flesh there on the
screen, and I began to envision smooth, vaginal flesh--having
some of my own--lubricants, silky hair, the pure erectile
tissue of these girls, like unbaked dough before becoming
pies; I thought of the positions to deepen the man's
entry, their buttocks firm as pears digging into the bed
or parted for the rear entry; I thought of confusion and
retribution and rage and craving, the pull through girlhood
to be woman, the woman pulling herself out prematurely;
I thought of the lewdness of it and the ecstasy, the stir
in the gut of naughtiness. Sweat popped out. I took a
swig. Oprah is not without her trembling crescendos. I won-
dered if, at their tender age--I was 18 when I first got laid--
they climaxed--I didn't and find it even now problematic--
if they well-pleasured--if climaxes hit them hard like
they do uninhibited women. I wondered if it was all
rebellion and how powerful rebellion-love could be. It
set me spinning. Oprah, as I say, is not without her *coup
de gras.* From the back row of the audience she produced--
presto!--a mother and her late-teen daughter, a former

teenage sex addict, formerly on this show, now diagnosed
with AIDS, a disaster and an object lesson. I pedaled on.
"Don't let your daughters do this," the mother pleaded,
"stand by them--do anything to stop them," and in the
distorted, elongated sounds before disintegration, cried,
 "She's been robbed of her childhood." Breakdown.
The guests looked on. The mothers appeared to soften
with tenderness--they had all evicted their girls--destructive
role models, evil beasts, but the daughters, leaning
heavily away, looked unscathed and further resolved with rage.

My wife and I debate this: sex is the dominant preoccupation
of the species with a smattering of love tossed in; sexual conquest
and submission overpowers the flesh and soul of practically everyone
in their public and seemingly cultured iterations; an unconvincing
veneer of garment covers consuming carnal conflagration without
which humans would be desiccated extinct mouthpieces. My wife
says no, I say yes, witness swaggering adolescents pumping themselves
full of alcohol-fueled courage in the face of colliding tendencies:
shyness and desire; look at adultery; look at the wailing manifesto
of singles culture; sample the monomaniacal content of popular
songs and literature. Behind every closed door blooms a climax.
My wife says mine is the attitude of the adult child of sexual abuse--
the insatiable hole mentality--that sex is a pleasure-producing drive
but that human is a complicated striver, pursuing companionship,
love, power, God, nobly and with dignity. I tell her addiction is
neither dignified nor empowering. She says I'm projecting; I
say, not now. She says we are not animals; I see the hyper-vigilant
creature crouched inside the flesh, like seeds inside an apple. She
rolls a spiral of pasta on her fork; I down some bread. I know
women, she says, whose lives do not revolve around man and
his little member, who are content attending events alone, or
socializing with friends, who while receptive to romantic possibilities
are not desperate; I say that experience has scorched these to the
point of exception, that they are rare sublimated creatures, that
women conquer men they fantasize about, and that they wield
equal sexual aggression and power, that woman is the head
of a match on fire, no less than man, the two striking equal in-
tensities from interior volcanic friction. We are both, by now,
uncomfortable, sucking in the room with emergent anger,
narrowing the light with intelligent antagonism. She accuses
me of sexualizing the world, of predation, exaggeration, of piling
up bodies of the dead in my terror of loneliness, and suddenly
I am aware of my underwear, my penis, my gluteus maximi,
my smile, the mechanics of my hands. I swig some water. I
try to focus the aperture of my mind. *The blinds are drawn.*
The walls are avocado green. The hard edge of the bed cuts
across my naked ass breaking me in half backwards forcing my
penis to the pinnacle of my pelvis high in the air. She has thick

black hair. I am giggling. I am six years old. My penis is like
a baby snail atop a smooth, round stone, a beautiful meal, and
just as my blood catches a ripple of exhilaration my lens blurs
as if smeared with Crisco and I remember not whether she
fondled me, my mother. I utter the terms primal directive,
genetically programmed, procreation, overplus. I don't know, I
say, and want to defuse the argument by kissing her in bed with
she dominant so that her breasts swing erotically through the air.

I lock my car when I go in the market fearing a rush
on my stereo; I deadbolt my doors at midnight.
I leave nothing in my athletic club locker but the
rags I wear most days, like rust. I sleep with a utility
knife beside my bed, all the windows locked at
starlight. Cassiopeia stretches in, but no gloved hand.
I know the crush of knuckle on jaw, know the
unrepentant desperation coiled, like a virus. My
sister's electronic security eye beams red while
she dreams of missed airplanes in vertical spaces.
Iron bars nullify my parents passageways. Alone,
I latch the window above the porch rail below
the second floor eve, neutering cat burglars. My
wife carries a whistle. Only I carry trash to the
dumpster at night at the back of the parking lot
beside the drainage ditch, glittering. I wear my
skin to protect my skeleton, and protect my brain
with my tongue. I know how to cock and snap my
arm through the shortest distance between points,
and how to rip off testicles, with a belt to prove it.
I eat paella at my friend's house under the eye
of a corner-mounted camera, and under the
same cold stare withdraw cash, purchase con-
doms, and glide the hall to my CEO. An air raid
siren which screams outside my house every
first Tuesday at 1:05 craves to scream again,
like a head on a stick. I have caller ID and a car
phone, and a car alarm system--don't touch--
and special door locks bent hangers can't
hook which I keep pushed down when I drive.
I quick-release from my locked Cannondale my
racing saddle and haul it with me, leaving a gaping
"o" in the tube. A steel box under the terrazzo
floor encloses my mother's valuables--emeralds,
pearls. The remainder's enclosed by a safe deposit
box. Whoever enters my neighbor's room trips
his non-technical alarm: two wire-haired terriers.
I step into the warm, crystal air, breathe, stretch
my arms in a V, shiver, free, free, and leave the
print of my joy in the earth underneath one sole
as I rock forward off my toes onto its counterpart,
alternatingly, into the land of fortresses and fortune.

The right side of me cries "fuck you!" to my left side
which continues, gloved and masked, packing explosives
into the drilled hole to blow the safe. My left half
flails at him, crumpling off his steely surfaces like a fly.
My right side slits his eyes, uncoils the fuse, hides, flicks
his Bic, Kaboom! Paper bills fly like a shot bird's
plumes. I reprimand, I scream--a siren--we take a leak,
one of our few collaborative ventures, others being
defecating, and occasionally, eating. My right side
refuses to shave, smokes cheroots, and participates
in disreputable scams, though he can be a dandy
in colognes and cashmeres--indeed, a fake. I have
put my faith in psychoanalysis, honesty, face-offs
with demons, restraint; he is all libido. We are like
a solid steel ball twisted in half, two flat walls which
once were fused. I thrash him and he giggles. He
thrashes me and I hurt, like skin. I can burn. Now
he mutters, "fuck off," and drags me into infidelity
against our wife. We enter her bedroom and bang
into action, throwing off clothes and sheets in the
pink afternoon. I scream like a crocodile's victim
rolling under swamp water, up and over, gasping
for air. He groans and pants as he fucks her from behind,
and she, also married, opens her vulva, like a pear.
This time it was urgent and she didn't come. We lie
in bed, stare at the ceiling, giggle, until he stiffens
again into iron and slowly she crawls on top and
comes hard, like a hull. I cry. I refuse the mirror
in which he shines. I am limp. We stride home, mail
in hand, to the pungency of dinner and wife. Abed,
we profess our love for her. Asleep our dreams clash.
Now I am holding hands with my right side in a chair,
and the world through our crystal and warring eyes
flows in with undisrupted beauty, pleasure, meaning,
hue--a rare blending--and we are at irreplaceable peace.

I don't want to appear sentimental, but I've got to tell you
there's something about food that breaks my heart, something
about spoons and forks, pastas and beans, something about
the eating which wrenches the human being of me, the way
the biology craves food, the way it spirals on a fork, the way
it fills a cup and glides down tubes, the way it cools, the way
it steams windows and nourishes, the way it gives flesh to
bone, muscle to flesh, strength to lift. I am not religious but
when I sit before food at dusk--rice or enchiladas or greens
or polenta--I suffer a little for the cave between groin and chest,
the ghost, the hungry gift, the grotto of acids, fluids, blood,
enzymes, song, love, and greed, the stream of magma; how
we pull all day, hammer and grit, care, strain, sing, distribute,
need, navigate cars, featureless, like in-the-shell walnut meat,
compose, and hope. Our mouths wrap around sandwiches,
mayonnaise, lunchmeat, cheese, tomatoes, our fingers hold
the spoon of soup, like weight and counterweight, soft balances.
Brain knows, stored in some back cabinet, the crucialness
of food, knows the embedded panic button in the blood,
synonymous with the President's red phone, knows the
proximity of deprivation and fear, the threat of callousness;
but somehow the refrigerator is always full, as if replenished
inexhaustibly through its back. Security! Forgetfulness! How
easy to reach for the tin of fish while plotting your next
slaughter on the market. Driveways, kids, and lawn chairs.
What breaks my heart I can't quite conceive--something to do
with tissue, thickness, continuousness, sponginess, ambition,
desire, pupils, the stretched-open hand, loneliness, children,
innocence, violence. Something to do with pendulums, opposites--
steel and down, fire and ice, night and light, rage and peace,
honesty and lies--but children most of all--adult and child.
Money covers food, food covers life, failure covers money--
paper, paper, scissors, knife. Something like that. Something
to do with grazing cattle, flipping tails, tufts of grass, blowing
leaves, cars whizzing by on interstates, the smell of dung and
prosperity, and the pendulum swooping back. I don't know. I
don't know. I keep envisioning the homeless with their placards
of distress at intersections beside traffic lights, dark humps in

ratty hats and parkas--Vietnam vets, schizophrenics, drug addicts,
blank stares, refuse, bodies like yours and mine, framed in bone,
wrapped by nerves; stomachs, lungs, livers, brains, parents,
kids, triumphs, failures, saliva, and tongues. That's not exactly it,
but the denial of it, the inoculation of work, the furious pre-
occupation of brain in the world, the arrogance of success,
the skin over sensitivity, the self-congratulatory soul on the
surface of the world in the plush of plentitude, the overpaid
aristocracy of President, Senator, Embassador, Head of State,
fatuous, on-the-take, duplicitous, transparent. The earth delivers,
keeps, inch-by-inch, pushing from its undepletable source an
ever-exchanging, imperceptibly giving off--like the tips of flames
or the ends of comet tails--nutritive thrill of potatoes, lettuces,
legumes, seaweeds, citruses, grasses, plankton, and wheat which
hogs, cows, sheep, and fowl, and unbelievable fishes, munch, gulp,
cross-cut, and rip to become food on our plates, simple piles of
food; it's not the brilliant nor the complex nor the cunning, nor the
lucky, nor the incessant yammerer at his desk, but the nobility of
food, the beauty of it, the pulsing hand, and the inalienable right to eat.

for A. G.

I wish I could have been there for my funeral, shaken hands,
thank you'd, drunk it in for the event it was: literary, social,
historical, the funeral of a poet. Dying was almost thrilling,
like falling asleep the eve before waking to Christmas glitter. I
almost believed I would rise from death, and feared it not. Unlike
others, my coronary, I felt, would be pseudo-fatal, my shutting eyes
a co-conspiratorial wink at God. That I did not awake, I'm in
disbelief. Already I am stiff, embalmed, and decomposing; my
jaw bones--those plowshares--have relaxed. But, oh, if I could
have been there to see my body in repose, my carefully arranged
waxen hands, and with my friends joined the procession and
the wake, heard the eulogies, shaken my head, chimed "what a
shame," and then gone home and lain with my lover hard-cocked
and exuberant, my body flaming into ashes on the other side
of town while I fucked him to Rachmaninoff. I always loved
crullers in the morning, and would have eaten one the day after
dying. Instead I'm learning the taste of my bones--my skull, my
tibias and fibulas, my shank, my pelvic bowl, my ribs and leg
bones all contorted and shoved into my mouth in the form
of ash at the bottom of an urn. Do they embalm the cremated?--
I taste an acrid chemical. I wish I could have stood among the mourners
and heard the panegyrics, the pulsing of my poems on the tongues
of grievers, felt the skins of drums throbbing with my lover's
hand in mine, warm, yeasty. I was loved like a god; I loved myself,
and wince at my self-abandonment, my onanistic bursting. Alive,
I jacked-off daily into the toilet or a towel to feel the power of
existence, the elasticity of living; an icing pulsed out that, were
it not for squeamishness, I would have eaten. Dismaying to be
a honey-hill on which ants teem, feed, and disperse, which is
a funeral. They will carry me to my favorite view and scatter me
to the wind. Already air erodes my consciousness, blowing
through me like radio static or gaps in the fuel; my gills feel like
they're melting and my opticals like their sprouting wings. Mother,
Mother, am I coming? Is this me upon the air? Is light shooting
through my mind? Am I an emulsion melting? I'm stuck on the
bony lobe of a cow, papery, wanting to blow, in the bowl of a butter-

cup, on surging waves, on dung, on a bumblebee soaring, on a thorn,
on glare, on a human lip, I'm over there holding the edge of myself,
flipping, all my greatness. They wept and hugged, it was in the
papers--essayists, novelists, reporters, old loves, consoled and let
go among furniture, incense, candle smoke, objects, all my books
propped against wreaths, open to sutras, odes, and villanelles,
and I was dead in my coronary, smaller than a child, wanting to
be held, a beautiful white gown surrounding me, like a bell,
fragrant, feet dangling, unbreathing, adored. Had I but this attended.

It's time for the humans to lie with the animals, for
the Dubuque-ian actuary on his tree-lined boulevard to
curl with the Dik-Dik, to enter her soft, white fur
with his swollen shaft on the jungle floor padded by
wheat grass; for the Washingtonian *Chef de Cuisine* to
slide off his pants in the Venezuelan sun and intermix
with the Cotton Rat, sucking its tail in his mouth,
like a string; for the Houstonian sewer & drain man to
wash his hands in Inner Asian sand and break his
semen bag in the red, open flesh of the Lynx Caracal.
It's time, I say, to destroy the human race by forcing
the Walla-Wallan personal injury attorney to spread her
thighs around the Howler Monkey, illuminating a whole
Guatemalan rainforest with her cries--time to dilute,
decimate, and reshape, time to intermingle the un-
speakable--to sodomize--to disassemble the ramparts
of fury and hate, and aggression wild as a chaparral.
Intel and Internet! Cell phones! The muscle-bound
cardboard Superman! Child abductors and gang hell! It is
time to reconstruct the species by crawling into the
animals--the apes, the fishes, the cloven-hoofed race,
the egg layers, and the sky-winged gods; the Tapir,
the Wild Ass, the Harbor Seal, the Caribou, the Tuco-
Tuco and the Antelope. We have desecrated the universe
with our homicides and flick-tubes, transforming the
beautiful back caves of skulls into garbage dumps.
Though it means condemning to oblivion the works
of Sergey Rachmaninoff, Theodore Roethke, Michelangelo,
it is time to plow under the whole rotted superstructure.
Perhaps they will sweeten the soil, neutralize the viral
coils of Gilmore, Bundy, Dahlmer, Speck, and the
innumerable rapists, killers, terrorists, pederasts,
torturers, fire-starters, and demagogues--starvers
all; perhaps they will fertilize the fields--Ludwig Beethoven,
Mahatma Gandhi, Leonardo Da Vinci, Sojourner Truth--
deliver blossoms into the sun. This is not poetry I admit, but
my indictment of the human race; reminiscent of apocalyptic mass
suicide, reminiscent of Kaczynski and his packages. You

may think me mad. It is time, I say, to cease birthing human babies so sweet and innocent in tiny shoes and thimble mittens, born on a wave of misrepresentation, and to go into the honest ones, thick of fur, noble, pure-hearted, wise, unwasteful, straight-forward, and dominated. Perhaps they will teach us humanity.

A bursting sun unrolls its morning flood through me.
Dipped in gold I scrawl love across this page. Suddenly
I am neither oblique nor mad, just a man in love with
his partner--meals together, talks, tandem sleeping,
the give and take of communion--the glint of gold over
everything. Lake in sun. Mirror. Water hovering
above cup's lip, like a cake of water. Today I will cook
oatmeal and wheat bran together, steaming, served
with milk, drink coffee opposite my lover whose hair
will be tangled still, from sleep, skin aglow before make-up--
we will discuss family finances and who will go to the bank
today about our loan, we will discuss my forthcoming
flight to Texas for my daughter's graduation, and her
graduation gift, we will mention the power of the
Red River and the North Dakotan flood, and perhaps
the Gingrich-Dole three-hundred thousand dollar loan,
the poverty of politics and politicians. The table, oiled
and rubbed from last night's company, will be drenched
in gold pouring in from the door. Our dead cells will
flake off us invisibly, will go about their dying, like a
secret comet's tail, beautiful to themselves, sparkling
off the core. Again the sun. It is a common day of exhaust
fumes and tempers, poverty and desperation, wealth
and arrogance, the usual explosive combinations, but
I am at peace, rising in brick oven-ness, loaf upon loaf
in my glowing soul, and know not why. Is just is. I
think of those images I have seen in photographs of
smelterers pouring molten steel into massive urns, how it
showers and splinters when it spills, and the steaming
veins and rivers flowing into molds--the men are poor
and powerful, but full of pride, so it appears, and the
steel they guide makes something strong. I feel like what
they've made before it dries, still gold and red and brim-
ming. If I am a beam shaped like an "I" to dangle from
cranes above a bridge, that's okay; if I am the cage of
a car, likewise. I am but a piece of things and my love a
part. Today the counter aspill with grains glows gold
under the window pane, each grain a boulder throwing a
huge flame of shadow and I, without warning, awake from
slumber's crumbling, am a heavy bowl, swaying and spilling.

I've stopped thinking about naked women so much.
Something fundamental inside me is shifting. I used
to think continuously of them, and when married
seized my wife through a dream to awaken inside
her--often. Now light beams break through holes in
my mind, like rotted cloth. They were a comfort and
distraction, naked women looming before my eyes,
sharpened me one way while dulling me another,
such that I cut myself on my own whetted flesh. Oaf!
What is happening? Is my brain migrating north
from the center where it was small but lethal, for
now I seem utterly listing, diffuse? Am I crawling
into my mind? I think of moles in their long gestation
underground, finally emerging into light. I think
of their blinking amazement. I am equally amazed
and dampened. I know not what to think about! I
loathe politics. Philosophy's too immense. I haven't
the lunacy to speculate on the cosmos. Naked
women have been my specialty; now they're
evaporating. There's just a colony of holes before
my eyes and dazzling light. I want to pull them
back, my naked ones--their navels, midriffs, toes,
breath--like an amputee wants his arm. What do
you do when you're subject's gone? I was gourmand,
connoisseur, master chef. My world's blank. I can't
think of a proper topic to fill you with. At what
point does a flower cease craving resplendence--
those bromeliads, calla lilies, magnolias--salting
the ground with brown petals? Is this a withering?
Am I a withering? Am I bleeding testosterone through
some psychic wound? Liquid yellow, gold? Am I
becoming woman? Am I dying--or chrysalis-like, being
delivered, finally, into something beautiful, the world
opening above my spine into a new profession of
love and transparency? I'm in transition. I'll wait
and see. All I know is my third wife's employer's ba-
by has captivated me--her baby smile, her spongy
cheeks, the way she grasps my finger, knee level,

and totters, chest out, like a queen. We go
shopping. All I know is unrelated disasters on the world's
other side wrench me. All I know is I'm not all fuck
and fantasy and man to naked women, braggart and
internally superior to my swarming rivals, and women
have transubstantiated into people. All I know is light
has crashed through some tunnel which dissolved, like
a wafer in its searing. Remember the little boy who
jumped in the milk and his crust of flour broke away
as he flew? All I know is something frightening and
sad is new and the word "screw" has broken into a
million pieces around my soul and bone structure.
When they loom now they are nude and embarrassed.

Another depiction of hunger in the newspapers, this one
a close-up of an African adolescent boy standing in line
beside a UN truck and breaking into tears for being so close
to food but not eating, of breaking into tears for being so close
to food but not eating, of breaking into tears in the middle of the long line
at which end lies milk, bread, oats, perhaps, I don't know, something, just
something to eat. The boy is so close he cries--he's a big boy, tall,
manly, masculine, hard, the boy cries through every cell of his body,
not through his brain or mind, not through intellect or outrage--
he is beyond that--but through the biological mouth of every living cell;
he has walked a hundred miles for this, taken a million steps, and now, just now,
it's too painful to be this close but not eating, not dipping his fingers in food,
not digesting and feeling the radiation. He is a face in a sea, not a face in an orderly
line, everyone there is starving, nearly dead, starving and begging with black outstretched
arms, sweating and banging inside, and the boy is so close, so close but behind a wall
and weeping--where are his parents?, where are his protectors?, where are the ones
who conceived him in damp places?, where are the cell makers?--dead already of hunger?--
sacrificed to get him this far?--who knows, the photograph doesn't reveal the nature of
relatives, just the desperation, frustration, outrage, and sadness. Enough cannot be said,
the injustices of our species, the empty political rhetorics, the paranoia and xenophobia,
the egotistical selfishness of ownership and artilleries, we all stand guilty in the face of this,
we all stand guilty in the face of this, guilty of division and subdivision, of baseness,
of blindness and stupidity, of pride and arrogance, and of godlessness, yes godlessness
among the faithful. This boy is the testament, in emaciated words, shaming us, like a father.
Give him food. Stuff his tears with wheat. Fill his penis again. Don't freeze him on film
in twisted pain, like a football play, this is not a sports hero, an embassador, a martyr,
it's a boy born into a framework, like rafters or subflooring, a blueprint he did not create,
and this in not Hell but Earth, wet, fecund, delivering, abundant, rainy, photosynthesizing,
yielding, oceanic, Earth, and there is no justifiable excuse for his starvation who has hopes
like your teenage son preparing for Harvard, or smoking dope. I don't know. I don't know.
I shake my head. With eyes closed I pound the keys of my machine in infantile egotism,
feeble of language, genius-weak, two dictionary pages in my blood to work with, to describe
and convey this horrific image, probably the thousandth like it I have seen, to someone, to you,
to my mate, to no one, perhaps just for me to bleed some of my top-heavy, overflowing
outrage into the street. I could compare, but I'm not. I could compare, but won't. I could
moralize but to what end. That would be the soul of fury, the uncontrollable flood of rage
unleashed to juxtapose affluent Westerners flinging sweat beads across Hard Rock Café
dance floors to this travesty, to this reeking portrait of humility. I won't do it. I won't harp

on American skunks eating better garbage in one night, their snouts in bags, than
men and women in whole dispossessed countries. Not that the earth is one organism, not that
people are interconnected, not that there is only one soul, not that you are me, not that
he is she, but that we are separated, shattered, disconnected individuals faring for ourselves,
battered with advertisements. Look, I don't know a whole fucking lot about African culture,
I'm an over-privileged Texas Jew who attended the university, whose mother painted her
nails, whose father drove a Cadillac, whose family owned a boat, whose pet dog
ate Kal-Kan, and who wore pink Chemise Lacoste polo shirts on tennis courts. I'm not
an authority on hunger. But I'm against this picture. It makes me sick. When I first saw it,
yes, I was on a Lifecycle machine in my new sport shoes at the athletic club and it shut me down,
it knocked my legs from their straps--how impressive!--I went rubbery. I looked around.
I saw, I saw, I saw again, I saw and saw and saw again. I got up. I sat back in. I re-slid my
feet into their pedals. I folded the image out of view. The paper was in quarters, small. But
the hand reached out to me. If this poem has lost its center, it's because, god damn, there is no
answer, the poem is hungry like the man, with no significant food to give, no hope or promise,
just a chaos of thoughts and words, like the throng, no satisfying conclusion, no baked bread
on its bones, no meat for skin, no flood of fluids in its cells, just a dry clicking locust of a poem,
boneless, but with a shell eating what's left of blasted plants, and glorifying itself before it dies,
catharsis-less, empty, a hive of words. I could donate a can of beans to something. I could
scrawl a small check to some humanitarian organization, I could drop my drop into the
starving bucket if it would help, and maybe I will, but I have no doubt that there will be more
pictures, more pictures, more pictures, a procession of deaths by starvation captured beautifully
by the Associated Press, passing through my life, my children's lives, and my grandchildren's
lives, ad infinitum, and that there will poems, like this one, a litany of poems extending
into the unspectacular future until there is no more humanity to lament and love, pouring
decentered, empty, painful condemnations from their helpless mouths.

Tightly, they backed the Ryder in, early morning, moving day, bouncing
it over the curb in the morning sunpour, and sliding it close as a
shave to a robin roosting on her eggs. She did not move. They
lowered the ramp. They hacked. They coughed. The dolly echoed
in the truck-drum as they banged it free. Stalwart she sat. She did not budge.
Have you ever seen a robin seal the nest with her breast? She looks
like water with a face poured in it. Instinct glued her to her nest. And
in the green expanse of grass across the street hopped her mate,
fussing, watching, alert as wire, thwarted from swooping to his low
condominium exposed by trimming, helpless. Wheels along the anti-slip
ramp clattered and squealed under the sideboard's load, the workmen
joked, their bodies popped like soda cans beneath the mass of the
redwood burl, they cackled and spit squirming the cadaver of a mattress
in, they drank and refreshed beside the steel walls thundering to the
touch. Fury fused her there in her crumple-bun of feathers, bead
eyes staring, proud as fire, and starving, I think, as her mate kept
trying without avail to angle in. We could have batted him with our
hands if he tried. And there lies a parable. We unwrap our things
in our new domicile--dishes, glasses, here's that basket!--from old
want ads, the funnies, front-page news--and place them in cabinets.
Try if you can to take it, my house, my wife, my instinctual plan
flooded with blood, I'll cut you in two and blow you away. Shave
my house close with your sinister van under moonlight and pry in, I'll
slit you with a blade. My feet hold me up, veined, nubbed, tendoned,
tough--do you imagine me a lump of dough when security's
threatened?--standing naked in my robe a coat of mail flows beneath
my flesh and above my bones. You may kill me and rape my
wife, plunder my property, prevail, but not without there being
blood and gore eight feet up walls. We rumbled and scraped
and shattered and banged, cyclopean, Colossus-like, god-statured, and
she sat and sat on her fragile blue architecture in plain view an arm's
length away with her mate screaming, and I am positive that were I
evil she would have battled my huge hand reaching in. I returned
days later in my whispering auto to the site of the slaughter to retrieve
odds and ends--pillows, blankets, the comforter--all was tranquil;
they were still there, this time he on the eggs and his mate on the
eaves, watchful, vigilant, preparing to drop down. And this is where
I left them, forever, to pile the few remaining things on my bed.

Watching professional ice hockey on TV, the semi-finals, Detroit
vs. Colorado--brutal, clean, elemental, fast, steel on ice, ripping--
the kind of thing I like to track, like a leopard in grass the
microscopic movements of its prey, like to pretend I'm tiger in
the blades calculating, watching, fangs tasting blood, like to
imagine I'm on my couch sublime, amber-eyed, sleek, and wise.
Never mind the commercials for beer or automobiles, those
false interludes, those insignificant blips between magnificence,
no bigger than grains, never mind mini-pauses in the beast
which flows. I'm a beautiful animal, efficient, quick, my brain
transmits down the length of my skin, this Saturday night wide
with silk flashes of heat, my mate in the grotto nearby soft
and ready on the inside. That's hockey, a tail of star-dust
following a puck-like-a-comet to the score-zone, wham!
I'm all cat and blood-in-the-heart of the players when suddenly
a dead squid wrapped in blue ribbon fills the screen, a wet,
veined, whole, big squid wrapped in ribbon dead on the ice
someone snuck in probably under his shirt and hurled there,
a proud ocean squid, glistening, maybe still full of eggs
or fertilizer, maybe wise. I know almost zero about squid,
but I thought of soft, grey-mauve sacks, of suction cups,
of syncopated pulsing through water, of ink clouds, of eyes
half-buried in slippery skin. I thought of the indignity of not
being eaten, instead being thrown into a stadium of screaming
fans after a propitious score, the scoreboard flashing WIN!
WIN!, eyes glassed over and tentacles lashed, the indignity of
ending up in an arena and then the trash, the waste. I stood
in my human flesh--bald tufts of hair, soft dick, clawless
hands--just rose off my butt, not panther, ocelot, cougar, nor
lynx, and, remote control limp in hand, looked at this jarring
sacrilege. What happened next is hard to explain. Forty-
eight years of advertisements flew through my brain: gleaming
teeth, shiny legs, silky hair, quenched thirst, needless speed,
satiation, dominance, self-righteousness, the whole sewer-
marketplace. I cannot say what I mean. Body parts appeared
before my eyes--lips, napes, knees, hips, tit-cleavage, flat
midriffs, like an oar-shattered lake, all swirled into a
grotesque human ball laced with TV's stupid predicaments,

situations, blowings away, exonerations, manipulations,
mechanical tittering, skits, extravaganzas, and routines.
And small explosions occurred on the surface of my
skin, eruptions through which broad shafts of light ripped,
stutterings and decompositions, burnings and
disintegrations, breakdowns of the internal circuit board
of me, profoundly, as if I were a melting lid around an
inextinguishable eye--clear, refusing--shooting rays of vision
out all sides of me, like a planet or transmission, a magician
in the universe, and I shut off, forever, a piece of my race.

Well, I heard of this convict who has permitted science to slice his
lethally injected corpse into single millimeter strips, every organ scanned,
muscle upon muscle, his body filleted into innumerable sheets thin as Kleenex
for the examiners, a CAT scan of his entire disinherited body. Rape won't
appear, homicide won't be seen dashing between atoms. We won't find
child trauma crying behind garages. But meat will glisten, like freshly
sliced veal, a Hubble scan of grain and ganglia, calcium and tissue, the
ultimate visible man. You could make a board game of this, a card game
of concentration, what strip follows strip, what strip yearns for strip, you could
award money for being close on an anatomical-geographical map: the Country
of Pulmonaria, The Cardiac Republic, The Reproductive Coast, your strip
draped over your arm, like pasta. The man died for his sins--rape, dis-
memberment--but lives inside the instruments. Well, it just caught my eye,
something I heard from a friend in passing, embedded in a wider conversation
about competitiveness, superiority, dominance, etc., the criminal lurking in my
mind after escaping her lips. Grotesquerie curls in the routines. If time
were a ground-to-sky wave pushing forward, while you in your circumscribed
space were down-shifting into first, elsewhere some technological saw was
subdividing a man whom they earlier froze solid. Now I am a literary agent in the
basement of my home with a bone-white phone, a flickering computer, pens
like bottle rockets in a cup, crammed book shelves, and, dare I admit it, a
stuffed Beagle pup. I rub my eyes. I feel the thickness of my hands. I see
my thighs aswirl with hair sweeping to my knees, and knee caps like helmets.
I sit in a chair, or wander up the hundred 2 x 4 boards builders years ago
hammered into stairs, to feel the sun, my fingers through my hair. And you
my love are somewhere...browsing, eating, day-dreaming, most likely
working, drawn around yourself, like a thief's bedsheet piled with treasure and
tied at the top, one beautiful piece. It's not enough to declare, "and round
and round she whirls in space," referring to Earth, like a colossus unfolding,
head in the sky, a stock response. We must return to this: a criminal who
willed his heft to science, the science itself, electronic saws, weird obsessions,
the immortality-drive, rape and dismemberment, the mackerel thrashing of too-
tight lives, the infinite capacity of the human mind to escape prison walls and
mundanity, the beauty of minutiae and the machinery to enter it, God, galoshes
and slickers within which to slip as we examine the blood-sherbert which was man.

She hacks the base of his arm, hacks and hacks with her
gleaming cleaver, pieces of flesh fly, like wood-chips, blood
pudding forms, but the arm, all muscle and will, proves
stubborn and thick, nothing like what she thought it would
be, a simple cut-through with a heavy blade to be done with
it. She was never a butcher, just a cold repressor. This
chopping off of limbs is much harder than stuffing
unpleasant feelings, they being non-corporeal. She raises
high her red-streaked blade and slams it down upon his
meat; muscle writhes, worm-like, contracts and gives, still
alive; no bone yet, that calcium shaft, just shoulder meat,
bull thick, endless, wearing her out as she hacks and hacks,
the hatchet extending her crooked arm overhead and flinging
cadmiums: clumps and strings on its downward path. Sweat
drips from her pits, her blouse is wet, stains spread, but
she is intent, even while wrist-cramping and panting
and uttering hellish vituperations, "fucker," "shit," "mine,"
"usurper," "violator," "penetrator," "male," curses hauled
from some unexamined pain-pool, and she being so pretty;
lily and sweet. The boy oblivious in his crib sings
tunes, mobile overhead, an ABC Play Station affixed;
the boy giggles, as, in another room, she strives to dis-
member the father's reach from him, her treasure-trove,
her bud-lipped. Persistence widens the inexpert, inevitable
V--remember diagrams in the girl scout book?--forming
in his shoulder; it groaned, a slit-throat sound, grave-like.
Not understanding, not drugged either, a complicitor, he
doesn't resist, the pain dull as she strikes bone, as if
vibrating a tooth's root to his shins, and not a handful of
shoulder. It takes two fools to ruin beauty. Amazed his
bone is rainbow color, amazing its opalescence, and
amazing to watch good-naturedly her grizzly chopping,
indeed, somnambulistically, to assist. Why not stop her?
Why not grab the boy and bolt? Why not seize her jugular,
this little lethal shrew, his wife? He ceased loving her,
anyway, the instant she delivered, yes. Now one blow
snaps the last underside bone-sliver, his arm hangs invertedly
and she saws with some new serrated instrument the triceps

through, and comes orgiastically--mutters, "daddy," "yours,"
"nobody," "mum," as from the shoulder his arm plops
against the floor, like a naked branch, comes, indeed,
in fact, vagina lolling and rippling ecstasy through
blood and brain, as, from her life and son, this betrothed
one, subterfuging killer, finally acknowledging her dominance
and his mutilated, dead limb on the floor, runs.

644

That you can't come is not my problem. I tongue your
button, slide easy in you, climb high your mound,
shaft opening hood, dart or thrust slowly, hold back
panting, but you clutch something other than my spine,
other than my shaft of breath, my love and desire,
something else, iron, a bar anchored down, muttering
"no, no, no, I don't love you, I'm melting!" There,
I am there against your hunger, touching gently, my
huge head coated, my spongy tip pulsing, and I pull
it out and again flick my tongue in and above your
hooded moon; you on your back half off the bed,
breasts thrusting out, nipples standing, my tongue
between your flung, bent legs, the monster boiling up,
breathing in the room, big hump, red, breaking through
the bed, "no you don't," you stutter half in pleasure
half in anger, and shove it back in and down, like
water after leakage, but I in male power keep after,
open my anus against lightning, fatten, relax, lighten
like a boat rocked by water, to rebuild your ardor, and,
yes, you stiffen, liquefy, narrow to a jerked compass
needle, the room dark chocolate, the world
waiting breathless, and up breaks the serpent, back
bulging blankets, ruby eyes shining, diving, rising
through the covers, hard, defined, frightening, cutting
across your back sidewise, and again your chords
form the word, "down, down." It is your father, your
brother, violent God, male muscle, hard fire, something
awful, and you wrap knuckles around a grate anchored
in concrete, refusing to surrender, and I, locked against
power, close the sphincter of my anus, narrow, solid-
ify, point my psyche Northward, and tired, explode
my web of waddage in you, my nebulae. If you cannot
come, it's not me you despise or love but some sinister-
fingered, heavy-sacked, internal bundle-maker. Bye-Bye.

I have been a traveler of inches, traversing
the exotica of my back yard, the black walnut trees,
the fuchsia horns, the carpet grass, the green crawlers
and hoppers near the ocean of rain pools. I have
flown the miles of inches with my portmanteau pockets
stuffed with personals--slips of paper, spectacles,
converted currency--traversed the countries of square
yards, mountainous or flat, dangerous or free, lain
under spiny canopy chipped with blue, gold, and gray,
fallen asleep in the Hungary of woods against my fence,
satiated with discovery. I have been a traveler of inches,
a steamer on ocean waves, far from home and equally
as poor having blown it all on geography, threshed
the wild mushroom shores of ancient Mesopotamia
under the stairwell of the woodpile, eaten the colors
thickly laid--reds, ochers, umbers, russet and green--
of wood, flickering, shifting through the lenses of my
eyes, alive; the white-blue wind streaming in ocean
tides, swirling off my long, brown waves near the
crab apple tree thick with buds, richly. Inches are the
exquisite extravagance of the world, oceans in a blade,
Moroccan sands, the clear white drop of nectar on
the tongue-petal, the soar of wing, the wild rushing
antelope along the jungle creases of brick and stone.
Patterns of death, skeletal, wintry bones sharp and twisted,
moon-glinted; deaths of Jews and Gypsies ten
centuries deep plastered on the Russia of vinyl siding.
I have been a traveler of inches on the jet stream
of my soles flowing in the sky over Ecuador, the
sheeting rain, the rainbows, the throaty calls, the
shimmer of throats, landed on bare earth on black
wheels among the reptiles, the pink bulging call and
snap-down, seen the monstrous predator on Pleistocene
legs slay and leave its prey's husk to the splitting
rays and grain-small claws. That is all. All I mean
until swollen again with travel-lust and resources,
parched for experience, laden with glistening
maps and instruments, I soar to new wild horzons after
the twelve vacationless months of drudgery
endured as the clock's huge hand falls between
centuries marking each new angle of the sun.

Half-gnawed, raw black walnuts zing from branches,
a perfect hail, thud the parched ground, hundreds
splitting air: it's squirrels! squirrels! in the canopies
robbing us of nuts, nut pies, nutty oatmeal, baklava--
industrialists against winter, building stores in the
potted plants and soil under petunias, great bulging
cheeks of earth. I look and they plop at my feet,
under rodent-barking and copulating, the trees shaking
with nerves. Well, after the first year of fallowness
I stopped expecting the trees to yield nuts for me--
in June I spy green nodes under leaves between
forking wood, and in July walk on a carpet of half-
eaten balls. Each bears the signature of squirrel plow
marks. Isn't that, as well, a symbol for love, leisure,
pain, exuberance, life itself--everything is half-eaten.
Yesterday on powdery, rocky, and sodden trails
I hiked nine miles through mountainous woods
stepping on deer tracks, horse hoof prints, and
human footprints obliterating them who will obliterate
mine piecemeal over time, in chips, knocking off
heel marks, toe thrusts, clean lines. Perhaps a mis-
shapen ridge of one step will survive years but then
the wind will take it. I am not whole in my skin--the
little nut of me--but whole in the stomach and gut
of the world, flung wide. Even at birth, purple and
new, I was but a piece she found to push through.
My feeling for you fragments, gives food, vanishes,
rains down, glistens, like flecks in fields of rich
ground, resurrects, nourishes with life what's all
around, fuses and detonates, separated by ripping
fingers of air. You may not close your hand
around it, solid and undisbursed, yourself disparate
but unhurt, until, finally, from above, your are
eaten into wholeness by the very God you love.

Fish scales filling the air, like sleet, and fish guts
under his high rubber boots on the cold, wet
concrete floor of the wooden hut by the wharf
where the fishermen drifted in on green sheets
of sea and emptied their bins of silvery gems;
scarlet-gilled, blue, pink, and red shimmering
jewels shot through his knife-wheel, the heads
white, and pink meat in cellophane sacks heavy
as lead the vacationers in Towne Cars and Coup
De Ville's carted home in ice chests to wives
and kids and the cat--tan, bald, freckled heads
and backs of hands, marked as beautiful as
the fish themselves before they were hooked
and hauled in under sun fists, flicking glinting
drops and convulsing on the fiberglass floors
of hostile crafts on the green-blue, salt laden sea--
the fish-scaler looking like James Dean in a
knife-blur, those golden locks shimmering with
flakes, flakes on his lips and brow, the knife
when ceased, a scimitar, razor sharp, the
butcher of fish, their down-curved mouths
looking dour, like gamblers peeling off hundreds
under pallid lamps dangling over felt tables,
and chewing down cigars--the hut of horrors
and beauty hovered by pelicans and gulls
looking for a swill, a little wriggling tail, and
feeding off spleens and roe sacks slid down
the wharf far enough to be safe for a quick
swoop-and-lift, the big yellow feet tucked
and trailing, like ballast, under greywhite
down to the tops of masts or severed pilings
stuck in water, like amputated fists covered
with barnacles and seaweed slime--and the
Oyster House where father slurped down
the uncooked eyes of whole lives from their
own slick body-cups full of Tabasco sauce
and salt, chased by soda crackers, he a Buddha
of sorts, slithering them down his slithering

throat opposite his shock-haired, young Jewish
wife when I was eight, nine, ten, and rich
with cousins, "the hoard," pouring through
this small intercostal town, like a scoop of minnows
wreaking havoc, important as mayors, to
the open air theater, the crashing rubber-rafting
shore, the pails of sand clams beautiful as
money, the market for jaw breakers and
gum, and the little hut on the wharf where
cousin Harriet mooned in love over the beautiful
blonde fish-scaler, like a single bladed windmill
or processor blurrily whisking freshly caught soft
cold animals to their ultimate biblical doom.

Now I am becoming invisible, my face flattening into
the nondescript much as any drywall behind flat white
latex, pictureless, without even a tack to focus on,
featureless, overlooked. In a coffee shop I am the
decor, what encloses philosophies and laughter and
sharp interjections, the cube and door and murmur.
I sit in my chair but fade, like a twilit tree in winter
mist, not even ghostly, just gone. In the steam of my
cup. No longer beautiful were I, rather, disgusting I
might command something, a glance, a notice, a
gawk. But to be just commonly diseased--pustuled,
papuled, incurably achned, with a rhinophyma nose--
is to be unseen and invalidated among the species.
How lucky were the Beast, the Phantom, the Hunchback--
their afflictions repulsed and gathered love
among the deeper, those for whom the soul
rides the lips, like wings upon slow currents of air--
who discover rapture in hideousness. Woe to the middling
ugly pushing along, the facially streaked, the
shatter-capillaried and medically diseased seekers
gaze through to their mates on opposite sides of a room
sipping ale, soon to be intertwined and loved,
bas-reliefed. They are the lucky ones. And the gorgeous!
Yes, the gorgeous! The faces which transfix. The
high cheeks. The sharp nose. The chiseled lips.
That indescribable combination of fawn-like features
which drives love mad, these are the twinklers
painful for the plaster-featured even to contemplate--
the unattainable. I rise from my table, papers and
novel in hand, amidst the conversations, the
hissing coffee machines, the slapping down of
coin on the happy counter, the coupled doves
touching fingers under the table by their hips, the
entering of players strutting their stuff--
the vicious gene pool--fling open the door, and
stream outside into the lower half of the hierarchy.

For an aphrodisiac Japanese *bon vivants* clandestinely drizzle
over delicacies an elixir extracted from the base of shark
fins--slam sharks on hooks, decapitate their fins, and slide them
back into the alien sea, rudderless, to spin downward into
mud, buried alive, like crippled submarines. See them whip
uselessly their strong bodies, live pop-bottle necks stuck
straight in sucking silt: shark + beauty - fins = hideousness.
While above, in the glint of Creme de Menthe and the distant,
irrelevant scream of an ambulance, an elegantly shod woman
internalizes a shark fin between her thighs; it wedges darkly,
churning blood around the edges, cuts the air pressing
her pubis into apple halves, while the man shark-hungry
shoves his bone in-between. Below sharks devour The
Broken One, teeming, burying teeth, yanking free meat-chunks,
whipping bodies, slashing their donor of ambergris, their
brother. The lady clenches her fists in the chocolate dark,
the one live piece of shark vibrating now under the man's
pelvis and shaft, the tray shoved aside, food half eaten,
the shark's fin wildly alive, smooth, black plate, silky rough,
broad-based, knees crooked, toes pointing to the sky
bringing in God, like a tuner, into the V with the small
shark fin at the base under the man's spine, while below
in the froth nothing remains but a slaughter of bones, soggy
meat, a blood cloud, an incident involving powerful navigators
and the decapitated. Satisfied, she falls into the pulverized
walls of her scrambled brain, like a heroin addict, her fin
retracted to a soft, unobtrusive ball, and the man falls
open into the hilarity and joy of indisputable domination.

The spook on my lap. The weird on my lap.
When I reach down to touch it my hand
comes up bloody. Two eye-slits, like a cat,
warm, breathing. Wants to be stroked, but
oft-times resents it with sharp teeth and
claws. Is thick, furry, loyal, sweet when wants
to be, but vicious when it shall. It sleeps. It
frolics. It prances. It leaps. It loves soft lace.
It loves balls with bells. It loves engorged
blood. It rarely leaves save to slake or relieve
itself. Otherwise it curls collapsed, adoring,
replete. It is my moon-pool, acurl; my baby,
helpless and, therefore, enraged. God made
it thus. God made it small, almost crawling,
humorously arrogant. With a pink mouth.
A gaping mouth in the center of its face,
with a rough or smooth tongue, depending,
full of love and hate, of opposites. Cold, hot.
Dark, light. God, emptiness. Has a throat
but don't touch it! Strangulation is its phobia.
Start with the entire surface of its face full
in your palm and slide all the way down
and feel it purr, your best chance against
malice, keeping a safe distance against
inherent defensiveness. The spook in my
lap, boy becoming man, lies on its back
upside down, soft as a trap, from which the
unsuspecting hand may come up bloody.

Each molecule of the sea is a number, randomly
connected into other numbers in all shapes and attitudes,
combining, colliding, merging and fusing, the sea a
googoplex of numbers, intermixed, overlapped,
forming an undulating organism, rising and falling,
swelling, swaying. Many a human has drowned in
numbers, inhaling 10s and 7s, their last appendage
a raised hand sliding under. The combination of numbers
form sea colors: aquamarine, green, copper, brown--
colors that weave one's breath into bursting, birds
loosed upon the air which are themselves numbers,
3 birds, 46 birds, 328 bursting birds, 2476 birds forming
a cloud whose molecules are numbers. Nitrogen,
hydrogen, oxygen numerals forming the sweet face
of a colt, a colossus, or cow floating, and metastasizing.
One cat sleeps on my lap, 2 squirrels quarrel in the
trees, 3 pans hang from metal hooks, 4 trucks wheeze
down the street. The tongues, lips, and teeth of
children at Eisenhower Elementary School form in
unison the sounds of numbers. Count to 10. Bob
can do it! Wendy can do it! Jason can do it, too!
Numbers bouncing off the walls, doubling back,
and filling classrooms, save a few which slip through
cracked windows, like ecstatic criminals. I love you.
You plus me equals love. 1+1=2 or 3 or 5, who
plus 3 generations equals 71. Fourteen people of
mixed gender wait on the curb in the year '97 or
was it '61? Mine is tied with a four-in-hand. Seven
steps, a landing; 7 steps, a landing; 7 steps, a landing;
every other one a 45-degree turn left to a door on
each of 18 floors counts the man with OCD. There
will be a minimum of 6 and a maximum 16 chemo-
therapy treatments beginning every 3rd Monday
and lasting 3 hours each. She died at 63 after working
40 years. The system on which I compose these lines
has 32 megabytes of RAM, a 4.3 gigabyte hard
drive, a 1.44 diskette drive, a 56 K fax modem, 4
megabytes of video memory, a 3-D virtual memory,
an AC-3 camcorder, a 600 x 300 DRI printer with
a 100 page sheet feeder, a 7 resistant fax, and a
266 MHZ Pentium processor. On the tip of
my last going-under finger, thrust high, 1 angel stands.

When the gut growled at the bank book; when
the enzymes cleared their ghastly throat; when
the esophagus roared something terrifying at
the empty pocket; when the intestines cried foul
at the scoreboard; when the white corpuscles
whistled to the shadows for assassins, and the
red corpuscles got out the chains and switch-
blades; when the occipital pulled out its hammer
and tongs and glared at the food pantry; when
the left ventricle valve phoned homicide after
reading the bottom line; when the cornea sodomized
the optic nerve and had blurry descendants, like
fertility-mud; when the bladder screamed
damn! damn!; when the lower python looked
for sludge to fill its gut and threatened with
soundless asphyxiation; when the urethra, looked
for steak in the Kenmore, pumped out hairballs
in a fit and took up the skull and crossbones;
when Amazon tongue rolled up like a useless
carpet after the Chief had long since passed
into his world never to return, and shot detumescent
bile jets into the cracks of its parched banks; when
the pancreas broke the glass and grabbed the ax
and with help from the spleen hauled the hose
to the safety deposit box full of worthless words;
yes, when the spinal column glaring one
last time at the empty jars and ended rolls of
Saran Wrap lying side by side, like dead soldiers
in a ditch, threatened to rip itself out whole
and crawl like a scorpion all night on my face;
I wept out into the world and looked for work.

718

I say to myself I am beautiful. I say come
sit by the fire next to me and I sit. I say
you have lovely hands, skin, and hold one
softly in mine. I say your eyes are like comets.
Night's coffee floods over us, night's blood.
I say in the firelight your hair looks like streaks
of wind flowing through and around trees
in white moonlight, like flight over Weeping
Rock. The flames flicker. Silence clambers
up our feet. I say I have only recently known
though we have long been friends--there
have been times I have actually hated you--
known your powers of loveliness, your root
and pulse sweet as sugar cane, have only
just understood. I say if I could only taste
and I put my hand to my mouth. Mmm,
I say, like bread, like life. I am afraid, I say,
so shielded, so laid in layers of protection,
muffled--yet, like a friend you tease me out.
I say I adore you as much as I have any one
or thing in my forty-eight years, and the
cricket of silence craws up our leg. Come,
I say, let me touch those teardrop muscles
running along your sides, let me taste your
thumb, and slowly I unbutton my flannel
shirt. Come, I say, let me feel, you are so
wonderful, the sheet of your hard-soft
tummy under my palm, and my unhitched
pants pop open. Yes, I say, and the fire
flickers. I say you have been suppressed
in an solid lead box. I say I value your
innocence, your honesty, your sorrow, your
life, slide my pants over the globe of my
ass on the white couch in the ten o'clock
half-light, and make love to one beautiful.

I strip the raised vein out my forearm by lifting it
whole with the blade of a knife and with it make a
ball of yarn I call my son. Like spaghetti spun on
a fork, thick and high and standing on its own wide
base, I give him eyes, a name. Allan I say, Allan.
The ball glistens red like tomato sauce. Say "Daddy,"
I command and feed him apricots. Say "Master."
The wrapped vein self-perpetuates and renews
by squirting and sucking in a ceaseless repetition of
sleep and food. Say, "I am your nemesis or life dup-
licate. I am your acolyte fashioned to echo your
productivity. I will assume the presidency." I
do not miss the vein that became my son though
it left a tunnel in my flesh for he is me watery and
splashing my stupendous trail. God love him.
God give him meat. Give him feet to incinerate.
I spin my child like a plate of vermicelli and he
quivers, smiles, accumulates--but then he hates,
the procedure awry, me, the plate, the fork, the
sea contained within the vein like a stiff steel pipe
of hell, he digs, he spits, he smolders, he flies, and
eyes two slit exposures of spite attempts to die.

Shoved his jeans into a back pack
plunked it on the steps, stuck on a note:
"You refuse my guidance, want it
your way, go to it." Imagined
him blowing me away, torching
the house, ripping me off for
boss narcotics, wiping baby tears,
screwed down tight by his own
folderol. My drop-out big shot
crack head con man with puppy
snout whiskers. Felt exhilarated,
cheese enchiladas, a Hollywood
movie floating above a chasm
of hell. Felt financially vigorous.
Want the cold packed earth under
a bridge where bums piss to be
his pillow, want a drill bored
through his gut, want the finger-
nail of crack to scrape the black-
board of his nerves, want him
back on bloody knees begging for
school or rehab, my angel boy in
the cherry red cap sticking his
fat in the Cheerios box, my Elton
John with pedal-fresh lips belting
out licks on the boutique's steps,
my Laurence Olivier, want him
peeled off rock bottom like a
gooey fruit-strip begging for dad
because I love his seventeen year
old ass more than he or I under-
stands, the way a man drowning
screams with terror for anyone
to save him from sinking into the
flat black mass, but no one swarms.

861

Son has tripped the light fantastic into temporality
shooting the crack and horsing about in burglarized
houses, a veritable pine Pinnochio in oblivion-land
eight balling and cataclysmically sprouting alien prongs.
He hallucinates among the rats and stars in the
corrugated bed of a pick up truck, uproariously
bouncing, like a Metallica riff. He has not brushed
his blades in weeks and his face erupts like Vesuvius.
Oh, the beautiful rage of teens stinging them off laws
like racquetballs. Mine has a feather of chest-cavity
hair, sprigs in nose, and a black dusting round his
wrists. What a joke to be a boy--gangly, hot
octopus laying over the mind, like a human palm,
shocking and sticking. You just hyperventilate.
See? Mine applies his mania to conning fools;
he can detach his middle finger and lay it bloodless
in the hand of man. He can weave a ball of hemp
instantaneously into a jumping god, and smile the
smile of UNICEF. Change flies from warm skin
into his cup. He's ordinary stuff like we only inchoate.
The strictures blunt their arrows on his chest. Sun
drowns son into a dot, then nothing, beyond texts,
body soap, and medicine, where on flaming sands,
prince of stones, he ponders the darkling emptiness,
where he may char into a black nest of bones.

862

The magnetized metal strip of you shimmers with energy,
indeed, your magneto vibrates voltage sucking me toward,
you pull the skeleton out my back as I race away leaving
an empty sack. Distant from you my bones stick to your
core like nails. See me dash. Pah! What a fool. I am all
slivers and pins standing stiff on you like a beard. Feel?
Make love to me. Push my steel back through my skin.
I am not cower, but ocelot who hunts with eyes flashing
forward, but when I fantasize leaping upon, my needles
rise on my spine like rudders. Sensitize. You swing me a-
round when I stray and stretch me across the latitudes
electrifying such that all my body hairs jerk, like a slammed
lightning bolt, toward you, toward you, my true north.

911

After binging on Dreyer's butter pecan in a period of
weight gain I went upstairs and almost forced myself
to throw up. I gazed into the toilet like Narcissus. I
imagined slamming two fingers down my throat till
a Vesuvius roared. I felt the weeping of my stomach,
and my accusatory belt. I wanted to kill the monster in
me, the cowardice, the unceasing executioner. Down-
stairs I heard the John Wayne movie: the charging
bugles, the beating of horse hooves, the swirling com-
motion of rifle fire and expiration, all muted by a series
of walls and corners, and in my soft cube, wondered.
I knew that finally I was tortured not enough to per-
forate the tissue of my gut, that I was still a bit of an
hibiscus, that I would rejoin unpunctured my partner
in the film. This brief lavatory interlude was brought
to you by Glamour Magazine, self hatred, pitiful par-
enting, powerlessness, and a rare form of male bulimia.

There shall be no more reading of fictional books; there shall be only transactions and the pursuit of transactions. There shall be a rising of the sea floor to shallow depths. There shall be no more teaching of literature to hungry souls until the hunger subsides and then vanishes from the lexicon of hunger. There shall be the paying of taxes and the paying of increased taxes through burgeoning incomes; there shall be the deadening of imagination. There shall be the redesignation of bookcases in the wake of an exodus of one population and the immigration of another, an epochal inanimate transformation. There shall be a certain indescribable shame paling the blood of the fragile young, their hands and fingers flat drained gloves; there shall be a general paling of the masses in favor of squeamish scientific empiricism, rational thought. There shall be no more reading of fictional episodes, but the practical exchange, the feeding or bleeding into the central stream or gushing river off which flow no imaginary tributaries. There shall be mechanical unsoftening titanium lips clicking against each other that shall be called kissing, and oil can frictioning of the central parts that shall be named lovemaking. There shall be the Internet paycheck with the tithe automatonically bitten off it, automatically redistributed, and not a single batted eye. There shall be a Not-God program formatted onto flashing disks sucked into lidded slots in the necks of worshipers each clutching in spot-welded hands the Global Enterprises, Inc. Edition of the Holy Book. Rather, strictly on beds of nails, there shall be no more sleeping on caressing syllables nor the arbitrary jungles of lush foliage rich with shimmering erotica streaming outward from spectacular heads.

1113

I have decided I will do this: I will eat my father.
I will cook him to tar and spoon the goo; I will
melt his shoulder bones into his buttocks and
watch his eyes boil like eggs. I own the kettle--
cast iron--and the site, a barn alive with mice and
bats, abandoned, dilapidated. I will stab him
severally, split his wishbone, and boil him til his
brain snakes through. Then the fun! I will eat
every atom of him over years until I have swal-
lowed, digested, and eliminated my father. I will
spice my meals with cranium filings. He will
reappear in the water supply as the rationale
for Perrier! After that who cares! Let them fry
me. Let them waste ink and trees. Let others,
righteous to the pips, over oatmeal, snap off
their lips long balloons of diatribe, the loyal
pets of their shoe-tassels waiting. I will have
achieved my goal, liberated to song, no longer
man but soul. Prosecute the doll of my body,
bloodhound me down, convict me like an SS
man, let the pellet fizz. You cannot kill God nor
an empty robe. When, in death, my neck caves
inward know that what passed through it in grainy
chunks, savoringly masticated, enspirited me,
peeled back filth to liquid gold, made me beautiful.

979897654321316549876554432213224650987098734124092387409138740129837401239287 40

192387540938256729458572102938304987123048723084720239857509876098317230984721 03

987472093874747109234701983745083496595435614356001894375029138474098567348916 75

490873402934708925704598740458731409587430589710485749887654313246798765465543 13

213134678973243213019837402918374273864812742084743093874021938657243652879789 87

654321316549876554432213224650987098734124092387409138740129837401239287401923 87

540938256729304987123048723084720239857509876098317230984721039874720938374745 857

210293847109234701983745083496595435614356001894375029138474098567348916754908 73

402934708925704593049871230487230847202398575098760983172309847210398747209387 48

740458731409587430589710485749887654313246798765465543132131346789732432130198 37

402918374273864812742084743304987123048723084720239857509876098317230984721039 87

472093874709387402193865724365287978987654321316549876554432213224650987098734 12

409238740913874012983740123928740192387540938256729458572102938471092347019837 45

083496595435614356001894375029138474098567348916754908734029347089257045987404 58

731409587430589710485749887654313246798765465543132131346789732432130198374029 18

374273864812742084743093874021938657243652879789876543213165498765544322132246 50

987098734124092387409138740129837401239287401923875409382567294585721029384710 92

347019837450834965954356143560018943750291384740985673489167549087340293470892 57

045987404587314095874305897104857498876543132467987654655431321313467897324321 30

198374029183742738648127420847430938740219386572436528797898765432131654987655 44

322132246509870987341240923874091387401298374012392874019238754093825672945857 21

029384710923470198374508349659543561435600189437502913847409856734891675490873 40

293470892570459874045873140958743058971048574988765431324679876546554313213134 67

897324321301983740291837427386481274208474309387402193865724365287978987654321 31

654987655443221322465098709873412409238740913874012983740123928740192387540938 25

672945857210293847109234701983745083496595435614356001894375029138474098567348 91

675490873402934708925704598740458731409587430589710485749887654313246798765465 54

313213134678973243213019837402918374273864812742084743093874021938657243652873 04

987123048723084720239857509876127420847430938740219386572436528797898765432131 65

498765544322132246509870987341240923874091387401298374012392874019238754093825 67

294585721029384710923470198374508127420847430938740219386572436528797898765432 13

165498765544322132246509870987341240923874091387401298374012392874019238754093 82

567294585721029384710923470198374508349659543561435600189434092387409138740129 83

740123928740192387540938256729458572102938471092347019837450834965957529138474 09

856734891675490873402934708925704598740458734965954356143560018943750138474098 56

432130198374029183742738648127420847430938740219386572436528730498712304872308 47

97898765432131654987655443221322465098709873412409238740913874012983740123928740
19238754093825672945857210293830498712304872308472023985750987609831723098472103
98747209387474710923470198374508349659543561435600189437502913847409856734891675
49087340293470892570459874045873140958743058971048574988765431324679876546554313
21313467897324321301983740291837427386481274208474309387402193865724365287978987
65432131654987655443221322465098709873412409238740913874012983740123928740192387
54093825672930498712304872308472023985750987609831723098472103987472093874745857
21029384710923470198374508349659543561435600189437502913847409856734891675490873
40293470892570459304987123048723084720239857509876098317230984721039874720938748
74045873140958743058971048574988765431324679876546554313213134678973243213019837
40291837427386481274208474330498712304872308472023985750987609831723098472103987
47209387470938740219386572436528797898765432131654987655443221322465098709873412
40923874091387401298374012392874019238754093825672945857210293847109234701983745
08349659543561435600189437502913847409856734891675490873402934708925704598740458
73140958743058971048574988765431324679876546554313213134678973243213019837402918
37427386481274208474309387402193865724365287978987654321316549876554432213224650
98709873412409238740913874012983740123928740192387540938256729458572102938471092
34701983745083496595435614356001894375029138474098567348916754908734029347089257
04598740458731409587430589710485749887654313246798765465543132131346789732432130
19837402918374273864812742084743093874021938657243652879789876543213165498765544
32213224650987098734124092387409138740129837401239287401923875409382567294585721
02938471092347019837450834965954356143560018943750291384740985673489167549087340
29347089257045987404587314095874305897104857498876543132467987654655431321313467
89732432130198374029183742738648127420847430938740219386572436528797898765432131
65498765544322132246509870987341240923874091387401298374012392874019238754093825
67294585721029384710923470198374508349659543561435600189437502913847409856734891
67549087340293470892570459874045873140958743058971048574988765431324679876546554
31321313467897324321301983740291837427386481274208474309387402193865724365287304
98712304872308472023985750987612742084743093874021938657243652879789876543213165
49876554432213224650987098734124092387409138740129837401239287401923875409382567
29458572102938471092347019837450812742084743093874021938657243652879789876543213
16549876554432213224650987098734124092387409138740129837401239287401923875409382
56729458572102938471092347019837450834965954356143560018943409238740913874012983
74012392874019238754093825672945857210293847109234701983745083496595752913847409
85673489167549087340293470892570459874045873496595435614356001894375013847409856
43213019837402918374273864812742084743093874021938657243652873049871230487230847

978987654321316549876554432213224650987098734124092387409138740129837401239287401
923875409382567294585721029383049871230487230847202398575098760983172309847210398747471092347019837450834965954356143560018943750291384740985673489167549087340293470892570459874045873140958743058971048574988765431324679876546554313
213134678973243213019837402918374273864812742084743093874021938657243652879789876
54321316549876554432213224650987098734124092387409138740129837401239287401923875409382567293049871230487230847202398575098760983172309847210398747209387474585721029384710923470198374508349659543561435600189437502913847409856734891675490873
402934708925704593049871230487230847202398575098760983172309847210398747209387487404587314095874305897104857498876543132467987654655431321313467897324321301983740291837427386481274208474330498712304872308472023985750987609831723098472103987472093874709387402193865724365287978987654321316549876554432213224650987098734124092387409138740129837401239287401923875409382567294585721029384710923470198374508349659543561435600189437502913847409856734891675490873402934708925704598740458
731409587430589710485749887654313246798765465543132131346789732432130198374029183742738648127420847430938740219386572436528797898765432131654987655443221322465098709873412409238740913874012983740123928740192387540938256729458572102938471092347019837450834965954356143560018943750291384740985673489167549087340293470892570459874045873140958743058971048574988765431324679876546554313213134678973243213019837402918374273864812742084743093874021938657243652879789876543213165498765544322132246509870987341240923874091387401298374012392874019238754093825672945857210293847109234701983745083496595435614356001894375029138474098567348916754908734029347089257045987404587314095874305897104857498876543132467987654655431321313467897324321301983740291837427386481274208474309387402193865724365287978987654321316549876554432213224650987098734124092387409138740129837401239287401923875409382567294585721029384710923470198374508349659543561435600189434092387409138740129837401239287401923875409382567294585721029384710923470198374508349659575291384740985673489167549087340293470892570459874045873496595435614356001894375013847409856432130198374029183742738648127420847430938740219386572436528730498712304872308472308847

978987654321316549876554432213224650987098734124092387409138740129837401239287 40
192387540938256729458572102938304987123048723084720239857509876098317230984721 03
987472093874747109234701983745083496595435614356001894375029138474098567348916 75
490873402934708925704598740458731409587430589710485749887654313246798765465543 13
213134678973243213019837402918374273864812742084743093874021938657243652879789 87
654321316549876554432213224650987098734124092387409138740129837401239287401923 87
540938256729304987123048723084720239857509876098317230984721039874720938747458 57
210293847109234701983745083496595435614356001894375029138474098567348916754908 73
402934708925704593049871230487230847202398575098760983172309847210398747209387 48
740458731409587430589710485749887654313246798765465543132131346789732432130198 37
402918374273864812742084743304987123048723084720239857509876098317230984721039 87
472093874709387402193865724365287978987654321316549876554432213224650987098734 12
409238740913874012983740123928740192387540938256729458572102938471092347019837 45
083496595435614356001894375029138474098567348916754908734029347089257045987404 58
731409587430589710485749887654313246798765465543132131346789732432130198374029 18
374273864812742084743093874021938657243652879789876543213165498765544322132246 50
987098734124092387409138740129837401239287401923875409382567294585721029384710 92
347019837450834965954356143560018943750291384740985673489167549087340293470892 57
045987404587314095874305897104857498876543132467987654655431321313467897324321 30
198374029183742738648127420847430938740219386572436528797898765432131654987655 44
322132246509870987341240923874091387401298374012392874019238754093825672945857 21
029384710923470198374508349659543561435600189437502913847409856734891675490873 40
293470892570459874045873140958743058971048574988765431324679876546554313213134 67
897324321301983740291837427386481274208474309387402193865724365287978987654321 31
654987655443221322465098709873412409238740913874012983740123928740192387540938 25
672945857210293847109234701983745083496595435614356001894375029138474098567348 91
675490873402934708925704598740458731409587430589710485749887654313246798765465 54
313213134678973243213019837402918374273864812742084743093874021938657243652873 04
987123048723084720239857509876127420847430938740219386572436528797898765432131 65
498765544322132246509870987341240923874091387401298374012392874019238754093825 67
294585721029384710923470198374508127420847430938740219386572436528797898765432 13
165498765544322132246509870987341240923874091387401298374012392874019238754093 82
567294585721029384710923470198374508349659543561435600189434092387409138740129 83
740123928740192387540938256729458572102938471092347019837450834965957529138474 09
856734891675490873402934708925704598740458734965954356143560018943750138474098 56
432130198374029183742738648127420847430938740219386572436528730498712304872308 47